Spring's Awakening: Embracing Renewal and Growth

Shanazs A. Khan

Introduction

Welcome to the world of Ostara and the Spring Equinox! In this guide, we will explore the history, traditions, and rituals associated with Ostara, as well as provide you with practical ideas and inspiration for celebrating this magical time of year.

To begin, we'll delve into the origins and cultural significance of Ostara, dispelling common misconceptions along the way. We'll explore the connections between Ostara and Druidic traditions, as well as its place in the Wiccan Wheel of the Year.

One key feature of Ostara is the association with Eostre, the goddess of spring and fertility, and the symbolism of the hare. We'll delve into the stories and folklore surrounding Eostre and the hare, and how they relate to the themes of rebirth and new beginnings during Ostara.

Eggs are another important symbol of Ostara, representing fertility and the potential for growth. We'll explore the magical uses of eggs in spells and rituals, as well as provide guidance on dyeing your eggs with natural colors.

For those who enjoy crafting, we'll share a variety of Ostara crafts and creations that you can make to enhance your celebrations. From an Ostara egg tree to flower crowns and crystal eggs, these crafts are accessible to everyone and can add a touch of magic to your festivities.

Setting up an Ostara altar is a significant part of the celebration. We'll discuss the importance of the altar, suggest themes and elements to include, and provide practical tips for selecting items and creating a beautiful and meaningful space.

No celebration is complete without delicious food, and Ostara is no exception. We'll share a collection of magical Ostara recipes, including deviled eggs, hot cross buns, roasted lamb, and more, that you can incorporate into your feast.

For those interested in magical gardening, we'll explore the concept of garden charms, old magic, and how to create a miniature greenhouse for planting Ostara herbs and plants. You'll also find a list of magical gardening plants and their purposes.

To enhance your rituals and celebrations, we've included a selection of prayers, invocations, chants, and dedications to use during your Ostara rituals. Whether you're practicing as a solitary witch or with a coven, you'll find spells and rituals tailored to your needs.

Finally, we'll encourage you to embrace the joy and energy of Ostara by engaging in activities such as dance, laughter, spring cleaning, and nature walks. These simple yet meaningful activities will connect you to the spirit of the season and deepen your celebration.

By the end of this guide, you'll have a wealth of knowledge and ideas to create your own meaningful Ostara rituals and celebrations. Embrace the magic of the Spring Equinox and let Ostara inspire you as you welcome the rebirth and renewal of the earth.

Contents

Chapter 1: Introduction to Ostara

When the light that is reignited at Yule, a festival observed by the Germanic peoples and linked to Odin, the Wild Hunt, and the pagan Anglo-Saxon Mōdraniht, balances and then overtakes the darkness, this signifies the time of the year that we know as Ostara. Many witches and pagans worldwide celebrate the eight renowned festivals represented in the Wheel of the Year.

Ostara celebrates the coming of spring and the Spring Equinox. At that time of the year, the sun moves across the line marking the equator. During that day, the day and night are balanced. They both last for equal hours of the day. In the Southern Hemisphere, the Spring Equinox usually falls on the 23rd of September. However, Ostara typically falls on the 21st of March, which is relevant to the Northern Hemisphere's Spring Equinox.

Spring comes to life when Saint Bridgit's day, marked as Imbolc on the Wheel of the Year, arrives. Non-surprisingly, the symbols that we associate with Easter and springtime, such as rabbits and eggs, are also significant characteristics of Ostara. Ostara, or Eostre, probably sounds a lot like Easter to you. Well, it does, and there's a very good reason for it. It seems that Easter started out as Ostara. The church Council of Nicea dictated that Easter would take place on the Sunday right after the first full moon that follows the Spring Equinox, in 325 B.C.E.

As we just mentioned, Eostre, the Celtic goddess of dawn, along with spring fertility, is celebrated through Ostara. The goddess' name happens to be very similar to the word "Easter." It also means "East," which is the direction of the sunrise. This is why this time of the year, along with its Celtic celebration, is ideal for goal-setting and action.

It must be noted that the popular celebration of Ostara has gone through various changes throughout history. Similarly, it had different meanings and symbols tied to it over the years. In fact, modern-day traditions suggest that the holiday celebrates the day that Pan, the Horned God, is reborn, and therefore gets to meet his consort, the goddess.

Another reason why Easter is thought to be derived from Ostara is that merriment and feasting are significant aspects of the celebration. This festival is also when people tend to conduct ritual cleaning, which helps them get rid of old, unhelpful patterns and make space for renewal.

The origins of Ostara date back to Celtic and Germanic peoples. The festival hails from stories that they used to share about the goddess. The spring equinox, also known as the vernal equinox, wasn't only celebrated by the Celts and Germanic peoples or even entire Northern Europe. In fact, the spring equinox is a significant occurrence in many countries and cultures worldwide, including India, Nepal, Portugal, China, Kurdistan, Uzbekistan, Egypt, Persia, Rome, Turkey, and Afghanistan.

The Ancient Romans celebrated the Hilaria, which were religious festivals that honored Cybele, the mother of the Gods. The followers of this goddess believed that she had a consort who was born through a miraculous virgin birth. The consort was named Attis, and he was resurrected every year following his death during the spring equinox of the Julian Calendar.

A pyramid called El Castillo, located in the Mexican Mayan city Chichen Itza symbolizes the alternation of day and night. This pyramid was dedicated to the Indigenous Mayan serpent deity Kukulkan. Each fall and spring equinox, the sun shines on the northern staircase of the 79-foot-tall pyramid and creates an illusion of a serpent slowly creeping on it during the late afternoon. The snake continues to go down the pyramid until it meets with a huge sculpture of a serpent's head, located at the base of El Catillo. For ten centuries, the indigenous Mayans of Central America have celebrated their own spring equinox festival.

To this day, many Persians celebrate the equinox as the new year or Nowruz. The Achaemenians, a Persian dynasty of kings, celebrated the vernal equinox with the No Ruz festival. No Rus translates into "new day," a celebration of renewal and hope, a common theme revolving around spring. Persians also celebrate the spring equinox with another festival right before Nu Ruz. This celebration, namely

Chahar-Shanbeh Suri, involves purifying homes and leaping over fires. It's incredible how these countries may have so little in common yet hold relatively similar beliefs about a specific period of the year. This just shows how incredible the coming of spring is.

In this chapter, we will explore the history and cultural origin of Ostara. You'll also find all about the connection between Ostara and the Druid's Alban Eilir. This chapter explains how Ostara is considered one of the eight sabbats on the Wiccan Wheel of the Year. Finally, you'll come across the key features of this holiday.

History and Cultural Origin

Have you ever thought about holidays and a Holiday? Well, it's safe to say that approximately each March 21st is a Holiday- a commonly recognized celebrated day. As you know by now, it marks the birth of spring and the end of winter. Not only is it the vernal equinox, but it is also Ostara. The vernal equinox and Ostara fall on March 21st this year.

Ostara, a pagan holiday, celebrates the day that serves as a global symbol of awakening, rebirth, and new life. Since the daytime and the nighttime are an equal length on the spring equinox, it is also considered a midpoint between the two extremities: light and dark.

The forthcoming spring celebration is a very popular practice among many ancient and modern customs across various nations and customs. Seemingly, Wicca has appropriated many of these beliefs and their symbols for Ostara. Like its counterparts, Ostara is associated with renewal, fertility, and rebirth. The time of the year signifies the start of a new agricultural cycle when farmers would plant their seeds.

Numerous symbols of Ostara are deeply rooted in other traditions. For example, the use of rabbits and hares, which we will delve deeply into throughout the following chapters, are examples of these emblems. The March hare was perceived as a symbol of fertility and spring in medieval Europe. This is because rabbits are a nocturnal species for most of the year. However, they come out in March, as it is their mating season, which is why they can be seen at any time of the day. Furthermore, female rabbits and hares can become pregnant with their second litter while still pregnant with the first. This should explain why they're perceived as a very significant symbol of fertility.

To celebrate the coming of spring, modern-day Wiccans and pagans typically go outdoors to meditate. They may also conduct a simple ritual that honors the occurrence. Others may plant seeds or include seasonal candy, like chocolate rabbits and peeps, as part of their familial celebration. This always helps get the kids in the spirit of the Holiday.

Common Misconceptions of Ostara

Ostara is probably the most misunderstood Neo-Pagan Wheel of the year holiday (more on that later). Many Pagans may not be aware that the popular concepts behind the symbolism and history of Ostara are based on speculations that lacked sufficient evidence that arose during the nineteenth century. Either way, one must keep in mind that it shouldn't matter if a specific spiritual practice is not based on solid evidence, as it doesn't strip it away of its spiritual significance. However, understanding the history of the Holiday can help clarify common misconceptions about the celebration.

The history we know of the Ostara today is rather gnarly. The roots of the Holiday can be traced back to the olden Proto-Indo-European days. But before we explore the origins of Ostara, it only makes sense that we touch upon the popularly held beliefs about this celebration. The most pervasive is that the goddess Eostre, which the holiday was named after, may have been an adaptation of Astarte or Ishtar. Astarte was the West Semitic goddess, particularly the ancient Middle East great goddess, and the deity of important Mediterranean seaports like Sidon, Tyre, and Elat. She was also thought to be the queen of heaven, which is why the Canaanites used to burn her offerings and "pour liberations" (Jeremiah 44). Ishtar is Astarte's Akkadian counterpart.

There are many stories regarding the association between modern-day Easter celebrations and Ostara. One of them suggests that the Easter bunny and eggs are adaptations of the Pagan symbols that represent fertility and are linked to the goddess Eostre and Ostara, which we will explain in greater detail later. It is believed that these symbols go all the way back to Ishtar. Others claim that the Easter bunny comes from an Eastern mythology hare. In accordance with this conception, modern-day Ostara celebrations choose to honor the Eostre and the coming of spring. They celebrate the fertility that appears in the vast lands of Earth, hence usually commandeering the egg and bunny symbols of today's western Easter Holidays.

The issue with either interpretation is that they're not historically based or evident. So, what do we really know about traditional Ostara and Spring Equinox celebrations, and where do our beliefs come from?

The Origins of the Holiday

Unsurprisingly, the Spring Equinox is significant among many ancient Eastern and Indo-European cultures and religions. The Babylonians, Persians, Romans, and others based their calendars on the spring Equinox being the start of the year. On March 1st of every year, an order of ancient Rome priests dedicated to Mars and known as the Salii held public festivals.

A spring festival known as Akitu was also prevalent during that time in Babylonia. Akitu surrounded the imprisonment and escapade of Marduk, a god, and his marriage to Ishtar the Earth Goddess. When he arrived at "Bet Akitu," Marduk started to celebrate with both world gods, the upper and the nether. He decorated a huge table with their statues during the event. He then returned to the city at night to celebrate his marriage to Ishtar. This was considered where both earth and heaven and the gods unite. The purpose behind the marriage was to bring this union to life by occupying the throne before everyone. They even recited poems on occasion. Their love was believed to create life during springtime.

Common Practices and Beliefs

Ostara is very closely linked to the Easter Christian Holiday. In fact, Easter is considered a variation of the equinox Holiday. Ostara and Easter, its posterity, get their names from Oestre or Eastre, the Teutonic goddess of Spring and the dawn.

Unlike Christmas, Thanksgiving, Halloween, St. Patrick's Day, and other common holidays, Ostara doesn't fall on a fixed day of the year. Depending on when the first full moon appears, Ostara generally falls between March 19th and 22nd of each year.

Ironically, most of the imagery and symbols that most Christians link to Easter actually originate from the ancient fundamental concepts, like life and rebirth, of Ostara. For instance, candy, bunnies, Easter baskets, eggs, and even new clothes are traditions that have been long devised with the Pagan holiday. It may also come across as a surprise to learn that painting and dyeing Easter eggs even dates back to ancient Egypt, where eggs were painted and eaten to celebrate the festival of Isis, the mother goddess. People used to gift each other painted eggs on the spring equinox.

Not many people know that the egg, which is among the most popular symbols of spring and Easter, is originally a very powerful symbol of life. An article in the Massachusetts Daily Collegian explains that according to Pagan legends, there is an incredibly horrible history behind the traditional symbol of Easter.

In old Europe, people commonly decorated eggs and offered them as gifts, as they believed that they would bring prosperity, abundance, and blessings around during the coming year. However, as Christianity spread and the "old religion" practices were abandoned, people began to hide the eggs and have children find them. Hence, the egg hunt game each Easter. This made all the children in the village look around everyone's gardens, fences, and other hidden spots at the same time. It was believed that people who sought out the heretics and heathens used to threaten children or bribe them with coins so that the person with the uncovered egg on their property gets accused of practicing the old religions. However, it's important to note that this is just a common piece of Pagan lore, and there is no documentation of this ever happening.

Traditionally, Ostara feasts include variations of ham and other meats. This goes back to the ancient celebrations of the holiday. People didn't slaughter animals during the winter back then, so they had to eat them sparingly. They also had to use a lot of salt to cure their meat. They did, however, welcome the spring season with fresh meat and an abundance of green options like nettles, asparagus, and dandelion greens. People ate them with zeal because they were easily accessible in the spring. Even in modern times, many Pagans prefer to eat sparingly at certain times of the year. However, they do it out of choice and not because it's a necessity. They eat a clean diet and avoid eating food containing manufactured chemicals and other toxins to maintain their health and purify their bodies.

Giving candy is a widespread tradition in the spring holiday, making the celebration popular with kids of all ages. The difference between Ostara and Easter is that many Pagans don't support the idea of rabbits dropping baskets full of candy for kids to enjoy. Instead, a fairy legend is widely exchanged. Parents tell their kids that it's only right to leave offerings to the spirits during the holidays to remain in their favor. So it happens that sweets are traditional gifts on Ostara. It was believed that if the fairies were not offered gifts, mischief would befall them.

Ostara and the Druid's Alban Eilir

If you think about the most prominent events that ancient peoples and cultures celebrated, you'll find that agricultural holidays are among the most significant. In modern times, the Druid tradition opts to create a Wheel of the Year that rebuilds a set of holidays more in tune with the changing seasons and terrestrial practices. This is why most druids celebrate the "Wheel of the Year," a group of eight holidays that happen every seven weeks. These holidays include the equinoxes and the solstices. According to the Druid Revival tradition, each has a unique name. The wheel also accounts for four fire festivals, which serve as the midpoint between equinox and solstice and vice versa.

If you wish, you can look up a chart of the druidic holidays or wheel of the year to get a clearer picture. The wheel of the year progresses from Alban Arthan (roughly December 21st), the Winter Solstice, and the time when darkness looms, to Imbolc. From there, it goes to Alban Eiler (the spring equinox), Beltane, and finally, Alban Hefin, which is the Summer Solstice (roughly June 21st), and when the light shines the brightest. Alban Arthan and Alban Hefin lie right across from each other on the wheel. Lughnasadh follows right after, then comes Alban Elfed (the fall equinox), then Samhuinn, and back to Alban Arthan. Alban Eiler and Alban Elfed serve as the two midpoints, providing balance during the year, making the light and dark equal. The other six holidays that we had just mentioned sit within either the dark or light halves of the year. Compost, growth, rebirth, and harvest are among the most recurrent themes and symbols throughout the Druid wheel of the year. Wiccan traditions have a similar wheel, which we will be covering in this chapter, in which Ostara takes the place of Alban Eilir.

As the celebrations of the wheel of the year begin, most druids start to feel a heightened sense of proximity to nature, as well as a deep appreciation toward the changing seasons. The existence of the Wheel of the Year, whether Druid or Wiccan, provides us with a sense of balance. It is a great way to keep track of the alternating seasons and the passage of time. This is one way we can pay closer attention to what we can learn from each season. The Druid Wheel of the Year is typically celebrated in different ways, either physically and terrestrial or through more mystical and spiritual activities.

Like Ostara celebrations, Druids celebrate Alban Eilir through food, gatherings, and grove rituals. They may also start planting seeds, helping other people out, participating in environmental cleanups, engaging in wildcrafting, writing, music, or painting, conducting a personal ritual, meditating, or reflecting.

Alban Eiler can be translated into "Light of the Earth." Like Ostara and Easter, this holiday is celebrated during the spring equinox. It is one of two "balance" celebrations. At this time of the year, Druids pay extra attention to the significance of planning, creating projects, coming up with new ideas, growing, planting, and nurturing. They view it as their shot to bring balance into their lives and realize the significance of harmonizing their activities in the larger landscape. They aim to remind themselves that they aren't walking the path of life on their own.

Ostara and the Wiccan Wheel of the Year

The wheel of the Year represents the eight Sabbats of the Wicca and Neo-Paganism movement. The Sabbats are holidays celebrated by pagans and witches worldwide through various practices. The sabbats are considered the eight pillars of the circle of life. In that case, that circle is an unending cyclical pattern of nature. This is exactly what the placement of the Sabbats on the wheel of the year symbolizes. Even though scientific breakthroughs have established that time is linear, we still can't help but recognize the cyclical essence of life.

You can think of the Wheel of the Year as a form of a calendar split into eight sections instead of 12 months. The Sabbats divide the year into eight equal sections, signifying the beginning of each season, and, as you already know, their midpoints. There are two categories of sabbats. The first one is the sun or lesser Sabbats, including Yule, Ostara, Litha, and Mabon. These, as we mentioned, are known as solstices and equinoxes, and they mark the starting of each season. In other words, the four solar or lesser festivals are the Winter Solstice, Spring Equinox, Summer Solstice, Fall Equinox. Other categories include the earth festivals, the moon, or Greater Sabbats. These are Imbolc, Beltane, Lammas, and Samhain. These signify the midpoints of every season. Unlike the first category, which includes Ostara, the moon Sabbats always fall on a certain day. You may have noticed that some terms are common or similar to the Druid Wheel of the Year.

As opposed to the modern-day Wiccan traditions and beliefs, there is no solid proof of an existing ancient Wheel of the Year, at least in its current form. However, it is safe to say that the Celts still celebrated the festivals marked on the wheel thousands of years ago. They were just as significant then as they are today, even if they were known by different terms.

The Wiccan Wheel of the Year goes as follows:

31st October - Samhain

20th - 25th December - Yule

1st - 2nd February - Imbolc

20th - 23rd March - Ostara

30th April - 1st May - Beltane

20th - 22nd June - Litha

1st August - Lughnasadh

20th - 23rd September - Mabon

The eight festivals or Sabbats were made to focus on everything that is continuously being obtained and then lost during the cyclical turns and alternatives of the years. In the ancient Egyptian civilizations, along with many others, the Celts thought that ingratitude was some type of "gateway sin." They believed that being ungrateful could lead to the darkness of resentment, pride, and even self-pity. However, these eight Sabbats force us to take a moment to observe and reflect on everything surrounding us. It allows us to express gratitude for all we have been given during the year. It also allows us to process what we have lost and make peace with it. It is the only way to find and maintain balance in ourselves and the world around us.

Key Features of the Holiday

By this point, you are undoubtedly well-versed in the holiday's symbols. Bunnies, fertility, and eggs are the symbols that come to mind when the word "Ostara" is mentioned. Besides the fact that we've been talking about these symbols for the majority of the chapter, we still have Easter and the continuity of this holiday to thank for Ostara becoming one of the most popular pagan holidays. Nonetheless, we are positive that you'll encounter some symbols that you probably had no idea about.

The Hare

The hare is among the most significant features of Ostara, and it is all for a good reason! The next chapter will teach you more about the connection between the hare and Eostre, the goddess. As we mentioned earlier, hares are also known for being a symbol of fertility, considering the number of offspring they typically have. Hares are also often associated with the moon.

Eggs

Eggs are symbolically representative of "birth," which makes sense, considering that many creatures lay eggs instead of giving birth. Eggs are also associated with the sun, abundance, and fertility. They are usually incorporated into rituals to help lift curses and make wishes in funerary rites and kitchen witchery.

Hot Cross Buns

While hot cross buns are a popular Easter symbol, they are also a part of the Wiccan tradition, as they have relevant significance to witches and pagans. They are also typically representative of the four elements of earth, water, air, and fire. Some believe they represent the major phases of the moon (dark moon, waxing moon, full moon, and waning moon) as well as the wheel of the year's four fire festivals (Imbolc, Beltane, Lammas, and Samhain).

Serpents and Dragons

The snakes come out of their winter hibernation during the time of Ostara. They roam around in the daylight, shed their skin, and lay their eggs. There are numerous reasons why serpents are easily linked to Ostara. The shedding is representative of birth and renewal. These creatures are also incorporated into several creation myths. Dragons are also symbols of Ostara, as they're associated with the worship of the sun and renewal.

Spring Flowers

Spring flowers make the ideal choice for altar decorations regarding Ostara celebrations. Many pagans also like to use them as offerings to their deities. Daffodils, celandine, catkins, crocuses, violets, primroses, and hyacinths make great spring flower choices. These flowers bloom during springtime and represent life, as they come around after long, harsh winters. Hyacinths make the most popular symbols of Ostara.

In the ancient Celtic culture and other various cultures, time was thought to be exclusively cyclical. It was apparent that the seasons alternated, and even people died. Yet, nothing was permanently lost because things came back around in one way or another, keeping the natural cycle alive. Springtime has also been one of the most celebrated seasons around the world, as it is associated with fertility and the agricultural season.

Chapter 2: Eostre and the Hare

Celebrations of the Ostara are intertwined with stories of Eostre and the Hare. This isn't merely a game of phonetics - all the words sound slightly similar, and that is because they share the same roots in Anglo-Saxon pagan traditions. To fully appreciate the magic of the Spring Equinox and why it has become such an important tradition for many Wiccan practitioners, it is important to delve deeper into its history and learn more about the goddess Eostre, from whom many of these beliefs have evolved.

More than Just a Name

According to German lore, Eostre is the Germanic goddess of the dawn, and she is shown in various writings and images as celebrating the Spring Equinox. In fact, according to the old Germanic calendar, the month most similar to what we now know as April was previously referred to as "Ōstarmānod," which roughly means "Easter-month." If you take a moment to re-read these words and say them aloud, you can clearly tell that they are related. Easter essentially predated the dawn of Christianity as a holiday and was initially named the Spring Equinox celebration.

To take it a step further and allow for the connecting of the dots, so to speak, we should devote a bit more time to Eostre and the iconography most associated with this goddess. In terms of symbols, she is commonly associated with the egg and the rabbit. According to legend, the goddess Eostre found an injured bird in the dead of winter, so she transformed the bird into a hare to save its life. However, there was one quirk: even though it was no longer a bird, the hare could still lay eggs and continue the feature of abundance and joy that serve to be markers of the spring season.

We will delve deeper into this fantastic story later in the chapter, but suffice it to say, many of the words or traditions common to the English language and Judeo-Christian in a broader sense have their roots in this pagan history. The connections are preserved in the linguistic asides and symbols humanity has maintained and cherished over the centuries. Further proof that celebrations of the Ostara bring us even closer to our shared history than previously thought.

The Goddess

Historians have recorded Eostre's unique story for centuries, and of course, there have been a few vagaries in between. Unlike other gods and goddesses we may be familiar with, an image of her visage was not used as often in Renaissance paintings or sculptures as, say, Medusa or Hercules. The few clear visual representations of Eostre herself - rather than the symbols she is often associated with - indicate a goddess with a benevolent face, flowers in her hair, and dressed completely in white. She stands in clear contrast to the wintry and dark image usually floating behind her. As a goddess meant to be an antidote to the cold and dark, she has often been represented as exactly that: generous, calm, and bright.

Eostre is a goddess often associated with fertility, spring, flowers, and all the elements that come to flourish in the wake of a barren winter. As previously stated, her name is used interchangeably with "Eastre," which has become known as Easter - without alluding to the goddess herself, of course - and "Ostara." Then, in the 1400s, under the reign of Charlemagne, Germans referred to her as "Ostaramonath." To avoid confusion when it comes to celebrating Ostara, the goddess will be referred to as *Eostre* in this chapter and throughout the book - though it does help to highlight the extent to which these traditions are so deeply intertwined.

For centuries, historians have argued about the origins of belief in Eostre. While there is a clear connection between her and Anglo-Saxon religions and myths, her name is rarely mentioned in popular literature. Again, the matter is complicated by the lack of a specific trace for Eostre in terms of her revival in paintings, sculptures, or works of art. In fact, her name appears in written records for the first time in the late 1200s, in a document written by St. Bede, an English Benedictine monk who lived at the monasteries of St. Peter and St. Paul in the Kingdom of Northumbria of Angles. Beyond that, her presence has primarily been felt through the linguistic vagaries people have held onto over time, as well as the numerous traditions associated with the pagan holiday that inevitably became part of Judeo-Christian folklore years down the line.

Unlike other gods and goddesses, the extent to which Eostre was worshiped in the same way as a deity is a bit uncertain. St. Bede, in his journals, had reported that pagan Anglo-Saxons in medieval Northumbria had held festivals in her honor during the month of April. However, beyond this formative text, we don't know much else about here and the extent to which the pagans honored Eostre. In any case, whether or not she was a singularly worshiped deity, by the 19th century, Eostre had become a huge part of German culture, appearing in much of its folklore and popular art.

Festivals for Eostre

Going by the texts that have survived, written by historical figures such as St. Bede, we have at least some glimpse into how the pagans honored Eostre. Unsurprisingly, festivals held in her honor are remarkably familiar to us now. Eggs would be brought and decorated, painted with bright colors and intricate drawings. There would be egg hunts and plenty of cooking because communal feasts were an important part of the holiday. Wearing flowers in your hair and creating floral wreaths for homes to inaugurate the beginning of the festival were de rigueur for all pagans who worshiped her.

Typically, bonfires would be lit in the evening before the major celebration would begin the next day. The following morning, water would be drawn from wells or the nearest water source, followed by a prayer to the goddess. According to literary sources, women - or young maidens specifically - were encouraged to wear all white to honor the spirit of the celebration. Much like it is now, Spring was regarded as a blank slate back then, a time for renewal and rebirth. Therefore, white and soft pastel colors have become synonymous with the season and Ostara in general. They indicate the rock, mountains, lush harvests, and the wealth of natural resources representing the ancient goddess. In turn, these are the colors we now most associate with Easter, acting as further proof that these things do not happen in a vacuum and that most current traditions have their roots in our shared history.

Besides the collective celebrations, pagans would create an altar in their homes and give thanks to the goddess of Eostre according to their own rituals. Smudge sticks were often used, just as they are today, and the prayers vary according to the personal preferences of the practitioners, but the baseline of giving thanks remains.

The Spring Equinox celebration includes a basic acknowledgment of the changes that occur over time. The ceremonies attribute these changes to the higher powers that manifest themselves in the form of the Gods and Goddesses. During this important time, the Gods and Goddesses of the Spring Equinox are sometimes referred to as The Green Man and Mother Earth. Yes, another way to refer to the Goddess Eostre has traditionally been Mother Earth. According to recorded history, the Green Man is typically said to be born of Mother Earth in the depths of winter, and he is then thought to live the rest of the year till the next equinox.

During the festivities, a woman and a man may be chosen to play the roles of Spring God and Goddess, play-acting courtship scenes and symbolically planting seeds. Then there are egg races, egg hunts, egg painting, and, of course, plenty of egg-based dishes to round out the holiday's unique festivities.

Story of the Hare

The story of the hare and how it has colored our perceptions of Eostre and Easter is rather interesting. While it is not exactly an ancient holiday, it is not a contemporary one either. Many people have erroneously perceived that the Easter bunny - or hare - is a product of the greeting card companies, like Valentine's Day. On the other hand, some believe the story of the hare and spring is as old as time, and it is one of our most ancient myths. The truth is somewhere in between. One thing is certain: the Easter bunny was never meant to be a rabbit; it was always a hare. It is uncertain why and how the hare transformed into a rabbit, even though the only conceivable difference is that the former are much larger animals, with long legs and ears commonly associated with popular depictions of the Easter bunny.

The essence of the origin of this story is that the goddess Eostre transformed a bird into a hare, who then responded by laying many eggs of beautiful, bright colors for her at her spring festival. While some writers claim that this story is incredibly old, others claim it was created as early as the 1980s. This decade arguably saw the nexus of the hyper-commercialization of the Easter holiday and the renaissance of the Wiccan religion.

Earlier in this chapter, the delineation was made between Ostara, the Ostre, and the Eostre - all words related to a similar concept. Many historians took St. Bede's word for it, believing the story of Eostre, an Anglo-Saxon goddess whose history is rarely, if ever, documented in pagan sources but rather appears in his own work documenting early Christianity. According to St. Bede and folklorist Jacob Grimm, who later expanded on the famed theologian's work, Eostre is a more localized version of a famous Germanic goddess named Ostara. St. Bede and later Grimm wrote extensively about Ostara - or Eostre - and how she was worshiped. Some historians have also pointed out that Eostre could simply have meant "east." However, this does not necessarily solve the mystery of the hare and the ways all Anglo-Saxon words share the same phonetic and linguistic roots.

According to stories written by later folklorists and archivists who have been trying to uncover the history of Easter, the exact story of how Eostre transformed a bird into a hare may be a bit convoluted, and there are different variations on the same theme. In all cases, a simple child's tale may hold the answer. This version will be summarized here:

Every Spring, the goddess Eostre would hold a massive celebration celebrating the end of the winter darkness. Animals and children the world over would gather to pay their respects to her and bring small gifts to express their appreciation for the change in seasons. One year, the hare wanted to bring Eostre a gift a day before the celebration was held, but it realized it had nothing to give her. It had been an especially difficult winter, and the hare hadn't been able to harvest much of anything and had barely enough to eat. While rummaging through the forest for some food, the hare found an egg in the grass, which tempted the hare considerably as they battled severe hunger pains. Instead of eating it, the hare decided that the egg would make a wonderful gift for Eostre since it symbolizes birth and the Spring season. So, the hare decorated the egg and prepared the present for the goddess. Eostre was so impressed with this beautiful object, with the selflessness of the act, that she decided from here on out that the hare would be responsible for delivering intricately decorated eggs to the world's children every spring till the end of time.

Does this sound familiar? Well, it should, since this version of the tale bears some resemblance to the more Christianized versions told later on. There is another way in which the story of the hare has been told and ties more specifically to the pagan spirit of things, as it were. Here is that version of the story:

The goddess Eostre celebrates the Spring Equinox every year by holding a massive festival in a lush, green meadow. One year, Eostre was late, and thus the spring season itself was delayed. This occurred because Eostre found a dying bird in the snow, which cleaved her heart in two. To help heal the bird, she brought it back to life as a white hare and named it Lepus. Eostre gave it the power to lay eggs for one day every year to pay tribute to the hare's original form as a bird. From then on, every year, the hare was allowed to give away its eggs to those attending the Ostara festival.

This version is far closer to what Wiccans these days celebrate when it comes to the Ostara. It is clear to see the ways Easter has evolved from this tale, and it's also clear to see how dear the hare is to the whole celebration of the spring. Eostre did not only bring a dying animal back to life, but she also transformed it. This story of shapeshifting reveals not only one but two magical acts of renewal key to our understanding of the entire season. Dying plants or roots in the ground are transformed into trees, flowers, fruits, vegetables, and so on. The connection is clear both emotionally and conceptually.

As such, it may be interesting to consider why the hare? Any other animal may have been chosen for this story if we are to take things strictly on a narrative basis. In reality, hares have always shown up as popular motifs in folklore, and they have been named time and again as familiars for witches, most probably because of their unique speed, which makes them difficult to catch. Some witches, such as the 17th-century Scottish witch Isobel Gowdie, have been documented as saying that they transform into hares when they need to escape.

Interestingly, in many other traditions, the hare is considered a moon creature, so its conflation with spring in Anglo-Saxon myth is rather intriguing. For example, the ancient Egyptians felt that the hare could easily switch genders during the moon cycle, making the animal a particularly androgynous figure. Likewise, in China, the popular adage of "the man in the moon" is replaced by "the hare in the moon" since the hare is seen to be a moon goddess's messenger. It is also tasked with guarding all wild animals, and it works to grind up the elixir of eternal life with a mortar and pestle. In fact, they are also tied to fertility in Chinese folklore since it is said that the hare can become pregnant by crossing the water in the moonlight or touching the rays emanating from a full moon. While it is surprising that the hare in Anglo-Saxon tradition is tied to the spring, the animal has always represented fertility and metamorphosis of some kind in the grand scheme of things.

Fact or Fiction?

There is little debate regarding the fact that pagans, druids, and Wiccans have always celebrated the Spring Equinox in one form or the other. The real debate is the extent to which the Goddess Eostre in all her manifestations - Ostara, Eastre, and so on - and the hare are real. Truthfully, Gods and Goddesses have historically served as conduits by which certain characteristics or difficult to pinpoint changes are made manifest in an easy-to-identify form. Therefore, the figure of Eostre may have been a way of communicating the significance of the spring season rather than an actual Goddess worshiped by the early pagans. Other folklorists and historians have pointed out that St. Bede may have simply misrepresented the festivities he witnessed centuries ago and misheard the word for "East" as "Eostre," but it is difficult to say.

Of course, this also means that the story of the hare is also quite debatable. While it is a beautiful story, regardless of the different versions out there, it may also be a convenient vehicle for expressing the uniquely transformative nature of Spring after a long, cold, and dark winter. Nevertheless, in history, the hare appears as an important animal for early pagans worldwide, and witches have historically looked to them as carriers of a powerful aura, one that allows them to take on altering guises in the face of fear or hardship.

What has never been debated is the fact that celebrations of the Spring Equinox are a constant in Anglo-Saxon tradition and world cultures more generally. While modern-day Wiccans are encouraged to pay homage to Eostre and tell the tale of the hare, it is only one part of an ancient celebration that has been taking place for centuries. The fact that some of these stories and traditions became a part of Christianity and the celebration of Easter is no accident: the Ostre has been an important part of our shared humanity for a long time, and the traditions, like other holidays celebrated by pagans, are difficult to shed because they are infused with so much meaning.

Chapter 3: Making Eggs Magical

Transitioning from the previous chapter, where you have learned about the association of the goddess Eostre with Ostara and the hare, this chapter will discuss how eggs are related to this topic. Eggs have been present as a symbol of Ostara in many Wicca and Pagan traditions, albeit the origin of symbolism goes far beyond the existence of these belief systems. The use of eggs in healing, protection, and spring celebrations has been present since the rise of Ancient Eastern cultures. An egg can be used for these purposes, raw and cooked. The shells can be made into powder - or in case of symbolizing the spring equinox - painted and decorated with different motives.

The Magical Eggs of Ostara

In many cultures, the egg symbolizes life, and some link it to the origin of the entire universe. In ancient times, members of clans exchanged eggs in the spring, which was thought to bring a plentiful harvest come autumn. In some cultures, eggs were given to be consumed in Eostre's honor, while in others, they were displayed in a sacred place of a home. Not only that, but eggs are considered to have magical powers, which are amplified at the beginning of spring when nature is reborn, and life begins anew. Eggs are thought to bring fruitful lands and chase away the dark part of the year. For this reason, they have been used in various forms to protect their owners or provide them with what they need in life. For example, in some Celtic and Pagan cultures, a red egg is given to newlyweds, enhancing their fertility.

But how exactly are eggs tied to Ostara? The answer to this question is twofold. For one, being the vessel for a new life makes eggs one of Eostre's most helpful tools for maintaining the fraternity of nature. According to the legends, Eostre's sacred hare has given her eggs as a gift. The hare presented the eggs in a nest he found them in, but he enchanted them with vivid colors instead of the usual brown or white ones.

The other explanation for the egg symbolism in Ostara is much more mundane and is related to the hare. Hares are creatures living in the wild, and before giving birth, they form nests to protect their young from the elements and predators. When the young grow up, they abandon the nests, and they are often reoccupied by plovers who use them to lay their eggs. When people found bird eggs in hare nests, the connection was attributed to magic.

The Use of Eggs in Magical Spells and Rituals

Eggs have been used by witches who wished to gain protection or heighten their powers for centuries. It is believed that eggshells can help rituals and spells come to fruition - especially during sabbats. Other creatures, including malicious spirits, can also use the magic of eggshells. To prevent these creatures from putting eggshells to use, a witch should either destroy their eggshells or protect them. The most common way to do this is by grinding the broken and dried eggshells down in a mortar. The resulting powder can then be used in protection, rituals including dressing candles for candle magick, casting circles, drawing sigils, carrying around spell bags, and much more. Throwing broken eggshells on the roof or placing them around the four corners of the house are also great ways a witch can protect their home from harmful spells.

Being a symbol of Ostara, painted eggs can be used in magical acts designed to appease deities and spirits. After the eggs are decorated, they are left either by the foot of trees or hung as ornaments on trees and other indoor plants. This ensures the home is protected, and its inhabitants will receive an abundant supply of everything they need. Another traditional way to use eggshells is making them into candles before Ostara. Burning eggshell candles during this sabbat results in similar magical benefits as decorating the eggs.

Dyeing Your Eggs with Natural Colors

In many cultures, decorating Eostre's eggs is one of the most common ways of celebrating Ostara. Feel free to try it out if you also want to pay homage to this sabbat by making your own colored eggs. However, for the magic of the eggs to become as powerful as it can be, it's recommended to use only natural color sources. Fortunately, there are plenty of magical herbs and plants that can be used for these purposes - and many of them can already be found in households. The items you don't keep in your home can be found in local health food stores or supermarkets. This way, the only thing you'll have to focus on is choosing which type of dyed eggs you want to make and letting your creative juices flow. There are two main types of dyed eggs: full and blown out.

Creating Normal Dyed Eggs

Originally, dyed eggs were left out in the open air to dry out naturally. Therefore, raw eggs were used for this process. If you live in a large home with a large garden or field attached to it, this may still be a viable option for you. However, if your only option is to place the eggs inside your home, you must cook them before decorating them. While some recipes require placing the eggs in boiling water to apply the dye, the eggs may not cook through during this process, so you may want to pre-cook them a little bit. Here is a step-by-step instruction on how to color whole eggs:

1. **Prepare Your Dye:** Take the plant material you are using for the different colors and place them in individual pots. Make sure you use plenty of them for each color. Pour water over them, add a tablespoon of vinegar, then bring to a boil. Let it boil for at least 20-30 minutes before placing the eggs inside. Check the intensity of the color before doing so.

2. **Prepare the Design:** While the dye is being made, you may prepare a design for your eggs. Pour vinegar onto a cotton swab, then rub the eggs with it to remove any grease that will prevent the dye or the stencil from sticking to the surface of the shell. If you are using them, you may create stencils from herbs such as rose petals, cilantro, or rosemary. Press the herbs on the eggs and pull a piece of pantyhose over them to keep the stencil in place. If you are using onion peels and cabbage leaves, you won't need to use a stencil as these will leave your eggs colored in different shades, which can be decorative on their own.

3. **Dye the Eggs:** There are two main ways to go about dyeing your eggs. The first is to take raw eggs and boil them in the dyed water. Slowly place the eggs (with or without a stencil) into the boiling dye, lower the heat and let them cook for 10-12 minutes. After that, turn off the heat and check the intensity of the colors. If the eggshells haven't reached the desired shade, leave them in the dye until they do. The second option is to place already hard-boiled eggs into a cooled dye and let them soak. This allows more control over the intensity of colors and ensures you don't end up with half raw eggs.

4. **Finishing Touches:** When you are satisfied with the color of the eggs, you can remove them from the container with the dye. Tap them dry with a paper towel, then let them air dry for a couple of minutes. Once they are dry, you can remove the stencil (if you used one) with a pantyhose and enjoy your colored eggs.

Making Blown Out Eggs

After dyeing raw eggs and letting them dry naturally, the next best thing is coloring hollowed-out eggs. Once their inside is removed, the eggshell dries much quicker. What's even more important is that you can literally leave these lying around in your home all year round if you feel like it. They can make for beautiful ornaments or decor items, and you can even give them away as presents to your friends and family around Ostara.

Blown-out eggs can be dyed in several ways. You can color them the same way you did the whole eggs - by boiling or soaking them in dye. However, hollow eggshells float, so you may experience problems keeping them immersed. One of the solutions to this problem is to simply color the eggs before blowing them out. Another option would be to place a strainer or small bowl over the eggs to prevent them from coming up to the surface. You can also get creative and hand dye the eggs instead of dipping them.

Whichever method you choose to dye the hollow eggs, blowing them out may take some practice to learn. Here is how to do it:

1. **Gather the Supplies**: You'll need a syringe or an infant medicine dropper, both of which are available at a pharmacy. You'll also need a pin and a paper clip.

2. **Prepare the Eggs:** Whether you are saving the inside for cooking or throwing it away, you need to clean the egg's surface before making a hole in them. Before starting, the eggs should be kept at room temperature for a couple of hours. You may want to put them in warm water for 10 minutes just before beginning the process.

3. **Pierce a Hole:** Hold the egg in one hand, the pin in your other one, and using a winding motion, make a hole in one end of the egg. Twist the pin a couple of times as if you were trying to screw it, push it in, then repeat the process on the other end.

4. **Scramble the Inside:** Take the paperclip and unfold it to create a longer pin. Stick it inside the egg and move it in a circular motion to scramble up the yolk. This will make it easier to remove it easily later.

5. **Squeeze Out the Inside**: Take the syringe or the infant medicine dropper and place it over one of the holes you have created earlier. Hold the egg over a bowl with its uncovered hole facing down, and start squeezing the syringe. The inside of the egg should come out on the other hole. You need to put the paperclip back again and scramble the egg a little more if it doesn't. You can also shake the egg gently to break the resistant yolk.

6. **Rinse the Eggs:** Don't try to get every bit of the egg out by blowing in more air because this could make your egg explode. Instead, fill up the syringe with warm water and squeeze this inside the shell. Shake the egg to make sure everything is washed off and blow the water out. Repeat the process if you need to.

7. **Let the Shells Dry:** Once hollowed out, you need to let the eggs dry at room temperatures for a couple of hours. Place them in an egg holder to keep them safe. When the eggshells are dry, you can keep them at room temperatures until you are ready to decorate them.

If you are dyeing hollow eggshells by submerging them in water, they will be filled with dye on the inside as well. After taking them out from the water, let them cool to room temperature, then gently blow out the dye water. When the water is out, let them dry a little bit more before getting crafty and adding a few more decorations to them.

A List of Natural Colors

Colors can have a powerful effect on your magic. They can even determine the success of your spells and rituals. Each color has its own power and can be used for different purposes. As you would use a color of candle or crystal for a particular spell or ritual, you can use different colored eggs to manifest your intention. Here is the list of natural sources and their symbolism:

• **Black:** While the use of plain black eggs may symbolize dark magic, there is no reason why you should decorate them with golden or colorful symbols. When employed alongside colorful protection symbols, the color black can be an incredibly powerful tool to ward off negative energy and malicious spirits.

• **White:** White is the most powerful color to use in magic. It can substitute any other color and has cleansing properties. Since there is almost no way to color eggshells white with a natural color, you may want to get white eggs to begin with and treat them as a blank slate. You may draw on them with any other color as you do on the black ones.

• **Green:** It is the color associated with nature; therefore, it symbolizes everything earthly and natural. Placing green eggs at the altar or space you are using can ensure you have the best start possible if you are trying out a new magic act. It promises abundance in everything you need in life to become a better human being.

• **Blue:** The color blue can help you get into a relaxed state of mind, making your practices much more successful. Blue eggs can be used to achieve clarity, so your intention is always well defined when casting a spell or doing a ritual. They may offer you protection or symbolize other creatures that do.

• **Purple:** If your magic requires you to tap deeper into your intuition, but you feel unable to do so, the color purple can help you out. Often associated with royalty and higher power, purple can elevate your spells and rituals to a whole other level. There is no better way to show off your creativity than dyeing your eggs purple.

• **Pink:** Using pink color is also a great way to show love. However, because it's more gentle than red, it may just be the perfect color for self-care. It can be helpful if you feel the need to be kind and more understanding towards yourself so you can heal from any past trauma and your magic can flourish once again.

• **Red:** While nowadays, the color red seems to be associated with passion, it was originally the symbol of fertility. Not only that, but red is the color that everyone loves receiving in gifts. If you want to offer protection for someone, you can simply give them a red egg. You can also use the egg to cast a protection spell for a specific person.

• **Orange:** Like yellow, orange can also brighten up your day. Dye a couple of eggs orange, and you'll also get your creative juices flowing so you can come up with new spells and rituals and find solutions to all your problems. This raises your confidence, further enhancing your magical powers, and you'll never get stuck again.

• **Yellow:** The color yellow can do wonders on lifting your spirit when you are feeling down and unsure whether your spells will turn out as they should. Painting your eggs yellow ensures that you'll always have sunlight in your home. It's the next best thing after going out to soak in the natural sunlight.

Natural Dye Sources

Here is the list of natural dye sources, along with the type of plant matter that contains them:

Yellow: Straws, onion peel, saffron, and dandelion flowers.

Orange: Goldenrod and Crocus petals.

Red: Plums and red beets.

Green: Moss, spinach, grass, and buckthorn berry.

Blue: Huckleberry, sunflower seeds, and logwood.

Purple: Elderberry or blackberries.

Brown: Walnut husk, alder cones, and coffee.

Black: Alder bark and walnut shells.

Pink: Pokeberry.

As with extracting natural dye for any other purposes, you can use hot water and vinegar to facilitate the process of dyeing your eggs. You can even make a batch of dye ahead of time and freeze them. The frozen batches of color can always come in handy if you can't find all these plants around Ostara.

Decorating the Eggs

You may leave your eggs the color they come out after being dyed. Some dyes will color the eggshells according to their natural pattern (similar to tie-dye), which means you'll already have some additional decorations on your eggs. That said, if you want to add a few more elements to them, feel free to do so. If you wish to use the eggs in a magic ritual, drawing sigils or runes on them can enhance their powers. The simplest way to add additional details to colored eggs is to use a different color to draw the desired symbols to your eggs. You can take a specific egg painting tool or a small art brush to make the small strokes. If you are good at freehand painting, you can do this without much preparation. Otherwise, you may want to sketch out the pattern you want to use on paper, then slowly repeat this on the egg with a pencil. Once the outline is drawn, you can proceed with painting the symbol.

If you want to use them as ornaments, you can add string, ribbon, or twine to them. You simply need to thread these through the existing holes using a large needle or a paperclip. These can also help you enlarge the hole to get everything through safely. Once the string sticks out on both ends of the egg, tie off one end, and decorate the other one. You can either make a simple loop out of it or add a few beads to cover the top hole and knot. This way, you'll have a much nicer egg to display for Ostara. Solid-colored eggs look the best with beads or small crystals added to them. If you are using the eggs for a spell or ritual, you may also want to add a charm or the symbol of the spiritual guide you are trying to evoke.

Chapter 4: Ostara Crafts and Creations

Since the Spring Equinox signifies the end of the winter, its celebration is usually a joyous occasion. All that greenery that awakens when the spring comes also reinforces the upbeat vibe of this sabbat. However, as with most holidays and celebrations, preparing for it can become quite overwhelming and stressful. Not to mention that sometimes the awakening in nature is still not visible yet around Ostara - or perhaps we cannot enjoy it fully due to our busy schedules. One of the best ways to remedy this is to create handcrafted ornaments and items that will remind us of the true meaning of Ostara. Even witches who are aware of the importance of performing mindfulness exercises can use these to focus and enrich their magic during the sacred sabbat of Ostara. Renewal, rebirth, fertility, hope, and balance are some of the most meaningful things in life in general. This chapter contains a few creations you can make to celebrate Ostara and brighten up your days even after the sabbat has passed.

Ostara crafts use items that can remind the creator about sunshine, spring rain, flowers, animals, harvest, and all the other beautiful things they can look forward to during those long months until the winter arrives once again. According to Pagan and Wiccan originating from Europe, the jovial nature of this sabbat is due to the extremely harsh winters people had to endure on this continent. People considered themselves fortunate if they could make it through the cold months, and once they did, they were more than happy to celebrate it. They thought being able to experience the inherent beauty of the warmer months is a blessing not to be taken for granted. They often spent the winter preparing gifts for Ostara to celebrate it when spring arrived. Plus, making the fun crafts had given them something to do during winter, as they couldn't tend to the fields, garden, or hunt.

Ostara Crafts Are for Everyone

It's no secret that those who dabble in Wicca and Paganism consider Ostara one of the largest celebrations throughout the year. However, you don't have to share these or similar belief systems to celebrate this sabbat by decorating your home. In addition, most people decorate their altar or the place they consider the sanctuary of their home. But feel free to bring spring into every room of your house if you want. You can even share the joy with your family and friends by preparing handcrafted and dedicated gifts for them for Ostara.

While you are probably familiar with the tradition of decorating eggs and making hare nests with eggs during this time of the year, there is so much more to Ostara than this project. Some of the creations you'll see in the continuation of this chapter were traditionally created by witches, while others aren't even witchcraft-related. Even if you aren't inclined to deepen your spirituality, immersing yourself in crafts can help you reconnect with nature. After all, spirits aren't the only ones who can generate positive energy. You also have the power to do this - and this power comes from nature itself.

Choosing Crafts for Ostara

Ostara is generally regarded as a celebration of nature and the awakening of the outside world, but it is also a celebration of possibilities. Crafts can symbolize your ability to achieve anything you want; you just need to find the right project for you. The selection of images, symbols, and items with magical associations you can encounter is vast. For this reason, finding the right project for you may prove challenging - especially if this is your first time celebrating Ostara.

In nature, many of them are born or reborn in the spring, making them the perfect choice for Ostara projects. All you need to do is find the closest piece of nature, step into it and look carefully for any inspiration. Grass, flowers, the sun, and even fruits and veggies grown in early spring can be included in your craft projects. Or, you can also add products and symbolism, such as eggs or anything else related to farm animals, wildlife, or otherworldly creatures. These are all connected to Ostara - and so are seeds, potted plants, or gardening tools.

When it comes to flowers, the most natural choices for this occasion are lilies, tulips, daffodils, snowdrops, crocuses, vervain, lilacs, carnations, daisies, clovers, lotus flowers, and violets. Out of the herbs associated with Ostara, your choice may fall on mint, dill, thyme, tarragon, parsley, tansy, lemon balm, rosemary, or lavender. Craft projects made for these can be used for various purposes, from candle dressings to protection spells to cleaning rituals. Furthermore, incorporating elements of spring cleaning can enrich all of your projects and inspire you to take on the task of beautifying your home with a much more positive spirit.

The color you'll be using is a matter of personal choice. Some prefer to use more earthy colors and even colder ones to signify the change in the outer land space from wintery to sunny. Others use brighter flower colors to remind themselves of the joyful nature of this celebration - and that life is just as full of possibilities as the color palette flowers come in. If you keep the finished products at your altar, you can also design your crafts to complement the aesthetics of the space. All in all, when it comes to choosing the Ostara creations you can make, the sky's the limit.

Ostara Egg Tree

As you would have learned from the previous chapter, the egg and its symbolism are the grandest hallmarks of Ostara celebrations. You were also able to see that there are various ways to color and decorate eggs and how plain ones can be used in magical spells and rituals. One of the projects where you can use your freshly decorated eggs is the Ostara egg tree. It does not have to be an enormous tree, nor do the ornaments have to be perfect. It will be sitting indoors, and apart from reminding you of the changing seasons, it should also symbolize the benefits of a new beginning. As long as you are having fun when preparing it, it will already begin to fulfill its purpose. And if you want to keep it on your altar, you should definitely keep the proportions smaller.

The Material You'll Need:

- Spanish moss
- Lightweight branches
- A vase

- Florist foam
- Acrylic paint
- Spring decorations

Instructions:

1. Decorate the vase or the pot with a design that reminds you of spring, such as flowers, butterflies, or eggs. Feel free to freehand paint the design, or even use your fingers to do so. The latter can be a ton of fun for children or any group of creative friends.

2. Allow the paint to dry before filling the vessel with florist foam. You'll need to hold the pot firmly in one hand and press the foam down so it molds to do inner walls.

3. Press the branches into the foam one by one and arrange them in a way so they will look like a tree. Use as many branches as you need to achieve the perfect tree shape and size that fits your space.

4. Once you are satisfied with how your tree looks, you can cover the top of the foam with Spanish moss.

5. Start hanging the eggs and the other spring decorations on the branches. You can also add ribbons and the cookie-shaped salt dough to the tree.

6. When the tree is completely decorated, you can use it as a tabletop or keep it on your altar. Or keep it on the table and only place it on the altar when you are doing rituals or spells.

Always use branches that have already broken off and not the ones still attached to live trees. The goal is to celebrate life and nature, not to destroy it. The only exception to this rule is the branches you get from pruning the trees. This procedure allows new growths to become stronger, so not only will you not harm the tree, but you'll also help it thrive.

The Flower Crown

In medieval times, flower crowns were worn by maidens who celebrated their youth, fertility, and springtime. Creating flower crowns is another way to bring fun into the Ostara celebration. Wearing them can help you feel more connected to spring on a personal level. After all, what could bring you closer to nature than wearing it? In addition, self-adornment is a great way to express your beliefs. And there is no better way to display how you feel than rocking a luscious flower crown with confidence. This will also enhance your powers if you are doing witchcraft.

The Material You'll Need:

- Floral tape
- Wire cutters
- 3-5 stems of silk flowers
- A piece of wire
- Scissors
- Needle nose pliers
- A thin ribbon

Instructions:

1. Start by cutting off most of the plastic flower blossoms from their stems. Be careful not to squash the flowers and leave a tiny length of the stem behind.

2. Use the pliers to curl both ends of the wire towards themselves until they almost touch each other.

3. Place a silk flower at one end of the wire and start winding a floral tape around its leftover stem. After that, wind the tape around the wire as well, so you can secure the flower onto it.

4. Take the next flower and repeat the process from the previous step, then do the same with the remaining ones until you arrive at the middle of the wire.

5. Move to the other end of the wire and start attaching flowers there as well, working your way back to the middle.

6. Once your entire wire is filled with silk flowers, you can tie a ribbon through each end of the wire. This will help you fit the crown to your head better.

Feel free to substitute the silk flowers for real or dried ones to make the crown even more true to nature. If you are using a real one, you can dry these later and use them in your practice. You can do the same if you're using flowers that are already dry, or you can preserve the entire crown for next year's Ostara celebration.

Spring Snake Wreath

As Christianity spread throughout Ireland Under St. Patrick's influence, it slowly pushed Paganism out of the country and the rest of Europe - an event that Pagans began to refer to as the snakes being chased away. They began to wear and decorate their homes with snake symbols to protest this. Nowadays, this practice has been reduced to wearing a small serpent pin on St. Patrick's Day and during the entire Ostara season. Those who more liberally embrace Paganism decorate their front door with a Spring Snake Wreath.

The Material You'll Need:
- A hot glue gun
- Rubber snakes
- A wreath form
- Spring greenery, such as ivy
- Ribbon
- Florist wire

Instructions:

1. Start by winding the ivy around the loop of the wreath. Be careful not to use too much greenery so you can have enough room left for the snakes as well.

2. Next, start placing the snakes between the greenery. When you are satisfied with their arrangement, secure the snakes to the wreath with hot glue.

3. Once all your snakes are in place, you can add a few more items, such as ribbons. You can just loop them around or make them into a bow and secure them with the florist wire.

4. Lastly, add a loop of wire to the top of the wreath to hang it up when all the glue has solidified.

Depending on the size of the loop, you'll need anywhere from 6 to 12 rubber snakes. You want to have enough of them to fully represent the message the wreath is conveying, but not so much that you can't add ribbons and the other decorations you are using to spruce the ornament up. Another tip is to pipe the glue to the wreath and gently push the snakes into it. Doing it the other way around, you would risk touching the rubber with the metal tip of the hot glue gun, which would melt it.

Crystal Eggs

Crystals have a unique energy and have been used for healing and protection for centuries. Witches can use them to enrich their magic or simply help them manifest the intent in spells and rituals. Crystal eggs are a craft project that requires baking the gems into an egg-shaped dough. The eggs can be used during the traditional Ostara games, which involve children looking for eggs the adults have hidden around their homes. When the child finds an egg and cracks it open, they will find the hidden treasure, which they can keep as protection.

The Material You'll Need:

- ½ cup of salt
- 1 cup of all-purpose flour
- ¼ cup of clean sand
- ¾ cup of warm water
- 1 cup of used coffee grounds
- Gemstones or crystals
- Cooking spray

- Acrylic paints

Instructions:

1. Start by blending coffee grounds, salt, flour, and flour, then slowly add the water and mix until well combined. You should end up with a thick dough.

2. Spray the crystal with cooking spray to prevent the dough from sticking to it. Take a small scoop of dough into your hand and put the crystal into the center of it.

3. Shape the dough into an egg shape and place it on a baking tray lined with parchment paper.

4. Bake the eggs at 350 degrees for about 12-15 minutes. Let the eggs cool after taking them out of the oven.

Depending on the environment you let them sit in, your eggs may take 1-2 hours to cool as the clay-like dough tends to hold on to heat. Once they have cooled, they will be rock hard, and you can paint them or decorate them as you like. After the paint dries, you can either display the eggs on your altar or hide them for the children to find.

Seed Packet Greeting Cards

With the arrival of the spring, it comes planting season. Even if you only have room for a few pots around your kitchen, there is something magical about growing your own plants. Seeds represent the promise of a new life, and by gifting them to your friends and family, you can bestow this promise to them. Seed packet greeting cards are a wonderful way to surprise your loved ones around Ostara. In modern times sending personalized greeting cards has become a lost art, but people who will receive yours will more than appreciate the gesture. Not only will they appreciate receiving a handwritten note from you during a sabbat, but the attached seeds will surely tempt them to try out gardening if they haven't done it before.

The Material You'll Need:

- Envelopes
- Pre-cut blank greeting cards
- Seed packets
- Pens and markers
- A glue stick
- Other craft supplies

Instructions:

1. Write a list of people you want to send a greeting card to, and choose a packet of seeds for each card.

2. Attach the seed packet to the front of the card. Use only a small amount of glue, so it wouldn't get onto the seeds but make sure you secure the packet so it can be handled safely.

3. Take a pen or a marker and write an upbeat message on the inside of the card. Feel free to decorate around the text with glitter and other art supplies.

4. Once the glue you have used is dry, place the cards into an envelope marked with the name of the person you are sending it to.

While giving seed packets for Ostara can be a great time to connect with friends and family, you don't need an excuse to send them a card or two once in a while to show you are thinking of them. Plus, seeds can be planted all year long. Birthdays or other momentous occasions at any time of the year could also merit sending these cards.

Cascarones

The tradition of making Cascarones for Ostara hails from Mexico. These hollowed-out eggs filled with herbs, confetti, perfume, or other items are also used to celebrate other holidays. Cracking open a Cascarone egg above the head of a loved one is said to bring them many blessings, luck, love, and happiness in the coming year. Pagan witches use a Cascarone during their rituals and magic spells for similar purposes.

The Material You'll Need:

- Craft paint
- A dozen eggs
- Tape
- Paintbrushes
- Material for the filling
- A funnel
- Tissue paper

- A wooden spoon

Instructions:

1. Take a wooden spoon and crack one end of the egg slightly open. Be careful not to hit the egg with too much force so it would break open completely. If you are going to use the insides, make sure to wash the surface of the eggs before cracking them open.

2. Let the inside out, then rinse the inner walls of the egg with water. Do this by slowly adding soapy water from a cup and leaving the shells to soak for a couple of minutes.

3. Once the eggshells are clean, place them onto a tray and leave them to dry overnight.

4. Use paint to decorate the eggs with magical symbols, or however you like, then let everything dry again.

5. Place a small funnel at the shell's opening and add the filling to the egg. Once the eggs are full, stick a piece of tissue paper into the hole to prevent the inside from spilling out.

6. Use tape, paint, and craft decoration to cover the crack, and your Cascarone will be finished.

The most popular choice for filling used by witches is dried herbs. Due to their magical affinity, herbs have a strong association with spells and rituals - and can be a useful tool for enriching your witchcraft. By choosing the right herbs and plants for their filling, Cascarones can be turned into a magic spell or become part of any ritual. Some options include lily of the valley, lavender, marjoram, thyme, lilac, purple clover, rose hips, and sunflower seeds.

Chapter 5: Setting Up an Ostara Altar

One of the joys of Ostara is that it's a season when many people choose to create an altar for their practice. An Ostara altar can be as simple or elaborate as you want, with the only limitation being your budget and time.

What does one need for an Ostara altar? A lot of creativity and a little bit of knowledge. That's all the supplies needed to create a beautiful, spiritual, and sacred space for this spring holiday. To build your own Ostara altar, you should have items from nature such as fresh flowers or fragrant herbs, candles in appropriate colors (purple is typical), crystals corresponding to the sabbat energies (carnelian may be a good choice), eggs, seeds, and other objects representing qualities associated with Ostara.

The Significance of the Ostara Altar

An Ostara altar is a physical representation of the spiritual connection we make to the natural world. It can be used as a place to focus our prayers and intentions and connect with the divine. The items on your altar should be chosen specifically for this purpose and placed in such a way that they create an aesthetically pleasing display.

When setting up your altar, consider the following:

- What theme or feeling do you want to evoke with your altar?
- Which aspects of Ostara are most important to you?
- What objects or symbols represent these aspects?

Ostara Signifies Balance

Balance is an important theme during Ostara. It falls on the equinox when the day and the night are the same lengths.

This holiday represents the balance of night and day, winter and spring, darkness, and light, culminating in rebirth or resurrection. In nature, it means that before we can have new growth, there must be dormancy as well - this is represented by the time between Yule (Winter Solstice) and Ostara.

The equinox is a time of transition, and as such, your altar should reflect this. You may want to include both dark and light elements or images of the goddess in her various aspects. As the season progresses and we move closer to Beltane (May Day), your altar should become more celebratory with bright colors and symbols of new life.

An altar is a place where we can work on our personal balance by honoring all aspects of ourselves. We can include both light and dark symbols and items representing the feminine and masculine aspects within us. The most important thing is to be true to yourself and create an altar that feels authentic for you.

Ostara Is a Time of New Beginnings

For many, Ostara marks the beginning of the new year. It's a time when we can set our intentions and goals for the coming months and begin to put them into action. An altar is a great place to start, as it provides us with a space to focus on what we want to manifest in our lives.

The items on your altar can be used as visual reminders of your intentions, and you can write these down and place them near your altar for daily contemplation. As you work towards your goals, it's important to stay positive and focused, and the Ostara altar can help keep you on track.

Themes for an Ostara Altar

There are many possible themes for an Ostara altar. Some of the most common are:

- Fertility
- Growth
- New Beginnings
- Springtime
- Joy
- Rebirth

When choosing a theme, it's important to consider the qualities you want to invoke during this time of year. If you're looking for increased fertility in your life, then an altar with symbols of fertility on it is one way to help achieve that goal. It's also important to make sure the items you choose for your altar appeal aesthetically and spiritually.

Choosing Items for Your Altar

When selecting items for your altar, there are a few things to keep in mind:

- The colors of the candles, crystals, and other objects should correspond with the energies of Ostara.
- Choose objects that represent qualities or aspects of the holiday that are important to you.

- Make sure the altar is aesthetically pleasing to you.
- Consider the space you have available for your altar and choose accordingly.

If possible, try to gather items from nature to use on your altar. This can include things like fresh flowers, branches, or leaves. If you're not able to get outside, consider using items that represent nature, such as pictures or artwork.

The Ostara Altar: Practical Considerations

Depending on your space and budget, an altar can be as big or as small as you want it to be. If you're looking for a place of honor in the home to set up an elaborate display, then consider one of these options:

- Create a permanent altar in a place of honor like your living room. This allows you to build upon it each year and continuously create new memories for your family.
- If space is an issue, consider setting up an altar on the ground floor of your home where everyone can see it as they pass by. You might want to set aside one evening per week (or more) to spend time at the altar and focus on your Ostara rituals.
- If you're traveling or don't have a lot of space, consider creating a small, portable altar that can be easily packed up and transported with you. This could include a few simple items like a candle, some crystals, and an egg.

How to Use Your Ostara Altar

Once you've created your Ostara altar, it's time to start using it! Here are a few ideas:

- Place fresh flowers or herbs on the altar as an offering to the natural world.

- Light candles and incense to create a sacred space for meditation and prayer.
- Set out specific items and focus on them one at a time.
- Place an item you regularly use (like your athame) in the center of the altar as a way to connect with it every day.
- If there are children in your home, consider placing toys or games on the altar for them to play with when they visit. (Just make sure to clear the items off before using the altar for a more serious purpose).
- Place pictures of loved ones who have passed away on your altar. Make sure they're displayed in an area where everyone can see them. This is a wonderful way to honor their memory during Ostara and beyond. Many people also choose this time to release any grief or sadness they may be feeling.
- Draw a tarot card every day from the Ostara Tarot deck and use it as a focus for your altar rituals.

Creating an altar is a wonderful way to connect with the energies of Ostara and create a sacred space for yourself during this time of year. It can be as simple or as elaborate as you want it to be, and there are no rules that say you have to use it in a certain way. Have fun with it, and let your creativity flow!

Elements of the Ostara Altar

As you prepare for Ostara, think about the types of objects that are most important to your holiday rituals. These could include:

- Pictures and artwork representing fertility – This can be anything from images of goddesses like Ishtar or Freya to flowers in bloom (such as tulips). The idea is to choose symbols that appeal aesthetically to you and make you feel connected to the holiday.

- Candles in colors that correspond with Ostara, such as yellow, green, or pink
- Crystals representing new beginnings, growth, and fertility, such as amethyst, rose quartz, or peridot
- Items related to nature, such as branches, leaves, or flowers
- Herbs and spices to add a scent that connects you with the holiday, such as cinnamon sticks, pine needles, or mint leaves
- Fresh fruits like pomegranates (to celebrate Persephone), apples (for their symbolism throughout history), or oranges (symbolizing abundance) – you can also use chocolate eggs, a popular symbol of Ostara.
- Anything else that feels special to you and has a personal meaning related to the holiday.

Here are some more details on colors, gemstones, and flowers associated with Ostara.

Colors of Ostara

There are a few colors that are associated with Ostara, and you may want to consider using them in your altar decorations:

- **Green** is the color of new beginnings and growth. It represents the fertile earth that is coming back to life after winter.
- **Yellow** is the color of sunshine and happiness. It symbolizes the bright future that awaits us all.
- **Orange** is the color of warmth and vitality. It represents the fires of spring that bring new life to the world.
- **Pink** is the color of love and compassion. It reminds us of the importance of giving kindness to others during this time of year.

- **Purple** is the color of royalty and magick. It represents the power and mystery of Ostara.

Using these colors in your altar decorations can help to connect you more deeply with the energies of this season. Have fun experimenting with them!

Gemstones of Ostara

There are also a few gemstones associated with this holiday:

- **Amethyst** is the stone of spirituality and healing. It helps to promote calmness and clarity during times of stress. This can be especially helpful if you're going through any major life changes at this time, such as moving or having children! If your usual coping mechanisms aren't working, try bringing an amethyst with you to help restore your peace of mind.

- **Aquamarine** is the stone of courage and intuition. It can be used to increase feelings of empathy in difficult situations, which may come up during this time if there are children or family members who have a new baby (or babies).

- **Diamonds** are the stone of clarity and truth. You can wear a diamond or carry one in your pocket to help you see things clearly during this time, especially when making important decisions about your life path.

- **Emerald** is the stone of prosperity and growth. It helps us develop new ideas that we may not have had before.

- **Rose quartz** is the stone of love and nurturing. It can be used to promote feelings of compassion in others as well, which may come up during this holiday if you're dealing with young children or family members who have a new baby (or babies).

Birch Trees

Birch trees are often associated with Ostara because they represent new beginnings and growth. It also signifies love and fertility. If you have a birch tree nearby, consider using some of its branches in your altar decorations. You can also use dried leaves or flowers from other plants to create a similar effect. A birch besom (broom) can be used to spread the energies of Ostara around your home.

Lavender Flowers and Sprigs

Sprigs of lavender are often associated with this holiday, too. Like other flowers mentioned in this section, they're commonly used for their scent during rituals involving love and fertility (such as weddings). However, these flowers can also be used to promote relaxation and peace of mind. If you're feeling overwhelmed during this time, consider using a sprig of lavender on your altar or carrying it with you as a talisman.

What Cloth to Use for the Altar

If you have a white tablecloth, that would be perfect! If not, try using a piece of cotton fabric in any color. White or off-white colors are usually associated with Ostara, and they can help promote peace and clarity during this time.

White Candles for the Altar

Candle Magic is commonly associated with Ostara. You can use white candles to increase the energies of new beginnings and growth mentioned earlier in this post (for example, by increasing your confidence or self-esteem). If you have a specific goal for which you'd like more support during this time (such as getting pregnant), try placing a candle on top of a picture or drawing of that goal.

The Importance of the Rabbit in Ostara

The rabbit is a symbol of Ostara because it represents prosperity. In some cultures, it's also seen as a sign of fertility. If you feel drawn to this animal, you may want to consider including a statue or picture of a rabbit on your altar.

Eggs as Symbols of Ostara

Another common symbol associated with Ostara is the egg. This represents new beginnings, growth, and fertility. If you're trying to get pregnant, you may want to decorate your altar with eggs (or use them in candle magic) as a way of increasing those energies.

How Long Should You Keep the Altar?

There's no right or wrong answer to this question! Some people prefer to set up their altar and then take it down immediately after the holiday has passed. Others like to keep it up for a few weeks or even months as a reminder of the energies present during this time. Some others prefer to only use it during certain rituals and celebrations, such as Beltane (or May Day), which is often celebrated around this time in various cultures across the world. It all depends on what feels best for you.

If you are using perishable items on your altar (such as flowers or fruits), it's a good idea to take them down after a few days so that they don't go bad.

What Else Can Be Added to the Altar?

There are endless possibilities when it comes to adding items to your Ostara altar! You can use anything that feels special to you and represents the holiday's energies to you. Some other items that you may want to consider include:

- Stones such as amethyst, rose quartz, or moonstone
- A pentacle or other symbol of the five elements
- Herbs such as lavender, chamomile, or mint
- Feathers from a bird you like
- A handmade (or store-bought) wreath or crown made of flowers and/or plant materials
- Pictures, statues, or drawings that represent your goals for this time of year, such as getting pregnant; it can also be fun to include pictures of family members who have passed on!

It's important to note that you don't have to use all of these items if you don't want to. You can also add personal touches and symbols

59

representing the energies, goals, or qualities you're looking for during this time of year! As mentioned earlier, the point is not really what's included on the altar as long as it feels right for you and helps manifest the qualities you want in your life.

If You're a Nature Lover…

There tend to be many opportunities for doing outdoor activities during this time of year, which can make it extra special for people who love nature and being outdoors! Try adding something related to nature (a plant or tree branch) to your altar if that sounds like you. You can also create a little vignette using items from nature, such as leaves and flowers that you've picked during walks outside.

Final Thoughts

What's included on your Ostara altar is up to you! The most important thing is that it helps you feel good and supports the manifestation of positive energies in your life. There is no right or wrong way to do things, so go with what feels best for you and enjoy the process!

Chapter 6: Magical Ostara Recipes

No celebration is complete without festive food. We can't celebrate a festival without serving some delicious mouth-watering dishes. Every celebration has certain dishes associated with it. For instance, can you imagine Thanksgiving without turkey? Is the 4th of July complete without apple pie? Certain foods make festivals, well, more festive. The Ostara festival is no different.

If this is your first time celebrating the Ostara festival, you probably want to serve some special dishes that will be perfect for this occasion. This chapter will bring you a few very delicious recipes that will make your guests rave about the food.

Many different ingredients go into making Ostara dishes. However, you'll find that some ingredients are used more than others, such as ham, eggs, mint, and spring produce. Eggs and Ostara share a connection because eggs have been considered a symbol of birth since ancient times. Christians were the first people to eat eggs during festivals like Easter, which they still do up to this day. They even make the eggs look more festive by dyeing and painting them. Therefore, to honor the spring festival, it makes sense to incorporate this symbol of rebirth and fertility in many recipes and eat it as a meal.

Ham is another ingredient that you'll find in many recipes. This is because our ancestors would use the preserved meat at the beginning of the spring. Another popular ingredient is mint, and it is incorporated in so many dishes because it symbolizes magic and wealth. Additionally, some people consider mint to have fertility energy, and its bright color makes it perfect for spring dishes. We will also use some seasonal fruits and vegetables in our recipes because they are abundant at this time of year. Chives are another popular ingredient because they have many benefits. They help lower your blood pressure and can be used as a remedy for ailments like lung congestion, cold, and the flu. Chives are also believed to be magical because they protect against diseases and evil spirits.

Recipes for Ostara Dishes

Deviled Eggs

Some people think that the word deviled is associated with or derived from the word "devil." However, there is no connection between the two words. The word deviled was first used in the 18th century to describe hot and spicy food.

We are starting with deviled eggs because they are incredibly easy to make.

Ingredients:

- 6 big eggs
- 2 to 3 tablespoons of mayonnaise (preferably full-fat mayonnaise)
- 1 or 1½ teaspoon of Dijon mustard (this is optional if you aren't a fan of mustard - either use less than what is in the recipe or not at all)
- 2 teaspoons of chives that are finely cut

- 1 teaspoon of apple cider vinegar
- Salt and fresh pepper
- Paprika

Instructions:

1. Boil the eggs until they are hardened. Since we are using large eggs, you'll need to boil them for about 15 minutes. However, if you want to use small eggs, then 9 minutes will be enough

2. Leave the eggs for a few minutes to cool down

3. Peel the eggs and split them in half

4. Remove the yolks from the eggs

5. Next, you'll need to mix the yolk with the rest of the ingredients - mayonnaise, vinegar, mustard, salt and pepper, and chives

6. If you are a fan of spicy food, you can add a small amount of tabasco to the mixture

7. Scoop the mixture and put it in the egg whites

8. If you want to add colors to your eggs, then you can sprinkle a small amount of paprika into your dish

That said, if you want the eggs to be pink, then boil them a day in advance and leave them overnight in beetroot juice.

Hot Cross Buns

Hot cross buns are a delicious pastry that people have enjoyed for years.

Ingredients:
Dough

- 3 cups of flour
- ¾ cup of sugar
- 1 cup of whole milk
- ¼ cup of melted butter or margarine
- ⅛ teaspoon of salt
- 1½ teaspoons of cinnamon
- ¼ teaspoon of allspice (this ingredient is optional)
- 1 cup of raisins (this ingredient is also optional)

- 1 cup of walnuts (also optional)
- 28 grams of dry yeast
- ¼ cup of hot water to dissolve the dry yeast
- 1 large egg, well-beaten

Frosting:
- 1 cup of orange juice
- 1 tablespoon of milk
- 2 cups of confectioner's sugar

Instructions:
1. Preheat the oven to 375 degrees
2. Combine all of the dough ingredients, except the hot water, egg, and yeast
3. Add the hot water to the yeast and let it dissolve
4. After the yeast dissolves, add the egg and the mixture
5. Mix them well altogether
6. After you finish mixing all of the dough's ingredients, cover it with a piece of cloth and leave it for an hour to rise in a warm place
7. Now that the dough is ready, shape them into round balls about 3 inches across
8. Place the balls about 3 inches apart on a lightly greased cookie sheet or a jelly roll pan
9. Now put the dough sheet in the oven
10. Wait for about 5 to 8 minutes
11. Open the oven and remove the buns
12. Using a knife, cut ¾ of an inch down into the dough and carve equilateral crosses on top
13. After you are done, put the buns back in the oven, and leave them to bake for about 15 to 20 minutes

14. When they turn to a brown-gold color, this means that they are done, and you can remove them from the oven

15. During the 20 minutes when the buns are in the oven, you can start making the frosting

16. Mix all of the frosting ingredients together and beat them until they are smooth and consistent

17. Add the frosting on top of the buns after removing them from the oven. It is important to drizzle the frosting when the buns are still hot

Sprout Salad

Now it is time to take advantage of some of the spring's delicious and beautifully colored vegetables.

Ingredients:

- 2 chopped green onions
- 2 cups of baby spinach
- 1 cup of mung bean sprouts
- 1 cup of alfalfa sprouts
- ½ cup of craisins and dried cherries
- ½ cup of slivered almonds
- 2 teaspoons of honey
- 2 teaspoons of Dijon mustard
- 1 can of mandarin oranges (this ingredient is optional)
- ½ cup of mayonnaise
- A dash of lemon juice
- Fresh dill

Instructions:

1. Get a plate or a bowl
2. Place the baby spinach first so they will be at the bottom
3. Next, add the sprouts
4. Make sure that you spread the sprouts on the plate so they don't get clumped
5. Sprinkle the dill, almonds, craisins, green onions, and the mandarin oranges (if you aren't going to use them, then simply sprinkle the other ingredients and leave this one out)
6. Now prepare the dressing
7. Mix the honey, mustard, lemon juice, and mayonnaise well together
8. Drizzle the dressing over the salad

We know that some people don't enjoy the taste of mustard so much. In this case, you can add any dressing you want instead. Additionally, if you aren't a big fan of mayonnaise, you can use less of the amounts mentioned in the ingredients. If you are leading a healthy lifestyle and don't want to use mayonnaise, you can opt for white yogurt instead. This dressing can also be a very delicious dip for chicken fingers that your children will surely love.

Roasted Lamb

After winter is over and to welcome the warm spring, our ancestors would prefer to have lambs as the first spring meal, making this dish perfect for Ostara.

Ingredients:

- 1 cup of white cooking wine
- 1 teaspoon of rosemary, chopped
- 2 cloves of minced garlic
- 2 teaspoons of olive oil
- ½ cup of orange juice
- Pepper and sea salt
- Leg of lamb

Instructions:

1. First, you'll prepare the marinade

2. Mix all of the ingredients in a bowl except for the lamb

3. Using a whisk, blend them together

4. Put the mixture in a plastic bag

5. Put the leg of lamb with the mixture in the bag

6. Leave it overnight

7. Make sure that the lamb is at room temperature

8. Take it out of the bag and put it in a roasting pan

9. Pour the marinade juice as well

10. Put the roasting pan in the oven and let it bake at 450 degrees

11. Let the lamb roast for about an hour

12. After it is done, remove it from the oven and put it on a rack

13. Cover it with a foil and let it sit in the marinade juices for about 20 minutes

14. Now, it is ready to be served

You mustn't overcook your lamb. When you take it out of the oven, the middle should still be pink. Additionally, letting the lamb sit in its juice for 20 minutes is essential to prevent the meat from drying out.

Mint Chutney

At the beginning of this chapter, we have mentioned how important mint is and how it is used in various recipes. Using mint in this recipe makes this sauce a great addition to various spring and Ostara meals. It can go with many dishes, and it is perfect for the roasted leg lamb that we have just mentioned. It can also go with bread, vegetables, spicy food, pasta, and Mediterranean food, or you can simply eat it with a spoon because it is that delicious.

Ingredients:

- 1 small, chopped onion
- ½ cup of cilantro, fresh
- ½ cup of chopped red pepper
- ½ cup of parsley, fresh
- ½ cup of chopped green pepper
- 3 cups of mint leaves, fresh
- ¼ or ½ cup of olive oil
- ½ teaspoon of sea salt

- A dash of lemon juice
- Water

Instructions:

1. Blend all of the ingredients until they form a paste

2. Gradually add water to the mix in the blender to thin the paste out

3. Keep blending the paste and water together until it becomes smooth

4. You can either serve it right away or put it in the fridge to serve later

Ostara Peep Ambrosia

Ostara peep ambrosia is a dessert that is very easy to make. It is the perfect dish for the Ostara celebration.

Ingredients:

- 2 cans of pineapple tidbits
- 2 cups of shredded coconut flakes
- 2 cans of mandarin oranges
- 2 bananas, chopped
- 1 package of 12 marshmallow peeps
- 1 jar of maraschino cherries
- 1.75 grams of cottage cheese
- 1.5 grams of any dessert topping

Instructions:

1. Cut the peeps into small pieces
2. Squeeze the juice from the fruits mentioned in the ingredients
3. Combine and mix all of the ingredients together
4. Leave the mixture in the fridge for a few hours
5. Take it out of the fridge and serve it as a dessert

Lemon Bread

Ostara is during the time of year when the earth is just waking up excited to welcome the spring. It is the time of year when beautiful vegetables, fruits, and flowers start to bloom. It represents rebirth. The lemon bread is perfect for this theme as it reflects re-emergence.

Ingredients:

- 1 package of any lemon bread recipe (prepare the ingredients on the package)
- ½ cup of dried cranberries
- ½ cup of golden raisins
- 1 teaspoon of orange zest
- Vanilla ice cream
- A ring
- A shiny coin
- A crystal
- A piece of silver or gold jewelry

(These last four items will be added to the bread as a surprise gift)

Instructions:

1. Prepare the mixture of the bread as directed
2. After everything is mixed together, start adding the ingredients
3. Add the golden raisins
4. Add the orange zest
5. Add the dried cranberries
6. Fold in the crystal, coin, or ring, making sure to wash them first
7. Whatever items you choose, they must not melt in the oven

8. Bake the bread according to the directions on the packaging

9. Take it out of the oven

10. Leave it until it cools down

11. Add powdered sugar or any glaze that you prefer (this step is optional)

12. Add a scoop of vanilla ice cream on top of each piece

13. Slice the bread

Before serving the bread, you should let your guests know that you have hidden gifts inside so they don't choke on them. That said, if you are making this bread for small children, you should opt-out of putting any treasures or anything in the bread that they may choke on. This bread can work as an appetizer or snack.

Roast Potatoes with Rosemary

Ingredients:

- 700 grams of new potatoes
- 2 cloves of minced garlic
- 2 tablespoons of olive oil
- 1½ tablespoon of chopped rosemary, chopped
- ½ tablespoon of salt

Instructions:

1. Add water to the potatoes, make sure that the water covers all of them
2. Bring the potatoes to a simmer
3. Cook the potatoes for 5 minutes
4. Heat the potatoes until they feel dry on the outside
5. Add the rest of the ingredients - rosemary, olive oil, garlic, and salt

6. Put the potatoes in a pan in one layer
7. Put them in the oven
8. Bake them at 180 degrees
9. Leave them for about 15 to 20 minutes
10. When they look brown and crispy, it means that they are done

Lemon and Lavender Cake

This delicious cake is perfect for the Ostara festival and celebrating spring's arrival.

Instructions:

- 2 eggs
- 1½ cup of self-rising flour
- 1 teaspoon of lavender
- 1 lemon
- ½ teaspoon of vanilla extract
- ½ cup of butter
- ½ cup of sugar
- ⅛ teaspoon of salt
- ¼ cup of milk

Cake Liquor Ingredients:

- ⅞ cup of powdered sugar
- 1.5 lemons, juiced

Cake Glaze Ingredients:

- ½ cup of powdered sugar
- ½ lemon, juiced

Instructions:

1. Preheat the oven to 355 degrees
2. Get a 8 x 4 loaf pan
3. Butter the pan
4. Get a large bowl and add the half cup of sugar and the half cup of butter
5. Next, add the lemon zest and the 2 eggs
6. Then add the salt, vanilla extract, teaspoon of lavender, and the 1½ cups of flour

7. Mix all of them together

8. Add milk to the mixture

9. Stir until the mixture becomes thick

10. Put the mixture in the buttered pan

11. Bake it for about 45 minutes

12. Before the caking finish baking with about 10 minutes, start preparing the cake liquor

13. Add the 1.5 lemon juice and the ⅞ cup of powdered sugar in a small bowl

14. After the cake finished baking, poke a few holes on top of it, and pour the liquor on the cake while it is still hot

15. Let it cool in the pan

16. Now, prepare the glaze

17. Mix half of the lemon juice with the 1½ cup of powdered sugar in a small bowl

18. When the cake is cooled down, you can spread the glaze over it

19. Decorate it with one teaspoon of lavender

Lemon and Herb Cauliflower

The lemon and herb cauliflower can be a great side dish for the Ostara celebration.

Ingredients:

- 3 heads of cauliflower (try to opt for different colors)
- 1½ teaspoon of thyme, chopped
- 1 teaspoon of chopped basil
- 1 teaspoon of chopped parsley
- ⅓ cup of olive oil
- ½ teaspoon of black pepper
- ½ teaspoon of salt
- 2 lemons, juiced
- 1 lemon zest

Instructions:

1. You need to preheat the oven to 425 degrees

2. Wash the cauliflower, then trim it

3. Chop the florets into small pieces, make sure that the pieces are equal in size

4. Put the thyme parsley, basil, and olive oil in a large bowl

5. Put the cauliflower in the bowl

6. Mix together

7. The cauliflower florets must be all coated with the herbs and olive oil

8. Get a large, rimmed baking sheet

9. Line the sheet evenly with parchment paper

10. Sprinkle the pepper, salt, and lemon zest

11. Squeeze the lemon juice

12. Let it bake for about 40 to 50 minutes

13. When the cauliflowers are done, they will become brown

14. Take it out of the oven

15. Sprinkle it with the chopped parsley

You can use other herbs and spices if you want to experiment with something different.

Spi nach and Feta Quiche

We have mentioned that eggs and spring vegetables are some of the main ingredients of many Ostara dishes. Therefore, combining them will make the perfect dish for the Ostara celebrations.

Ingredients:
Crust:

- 215 grams of all-purpose flours
- 3 tablespoons of cold water
- ¾ of kosher salt
- 170 grams of diced cold unsalted butter

Filling:

- 6 large eggs
- ¾ cup of soft cream cheese (make sure that it is room temperature)
- 283 grams of frozen chopped spinach, thawed
- ⅓ cup of each heavy cream and whole milk

- 100 grams of goat feta
- 1 teaspoon of kosher salt
- 1 cup of grated cheddar
- ½ teaspoon of ground black pepper
- 8 thinly sliced green onions
- ½ cup of grated Parmesan cheese
- Non-stick spray oil

Instructions:
Crust:

1. Blend the salt and flour in a food processor
2. Add butter
3. Add water while the machine is running
4. Stop once the dough is balled
5. Next, wrap the dough in plastic paper and put it in the freezer
6. Leave it for about 15 to 20 minutes
7. You want the dough to be firm, not hard
8. Get a 9x13 inch pan
9. Coat it lightly with oil
10. Add parchment paper at the bottom
11. Place the dough in the pan and press it in an even layer
12. Press the dough all around and let it extend a little over the edge of the pan
13. Now put the dough in the freezer again for about 20 minutes until it becomes solid

Filling:

1. Preheat the oven to 425 degrees
2. Get a large sheet of foil and coat it lightly with spray oil

3. Wait until the crust becomes solid

4. Then prick the crust using a fork and press the oiled side of the foil down against the dough

5. Fill the crust with rice, pie weights, or dried beans

6. Let it bake for about 20 minutes

7. Remove the weights and foil slowly and gently

8. Put it back in the oven and let it bake for 5 minutes or more

9. Now, prepare the filling using a whisk or an eclectic mixer

10. Beat the cream cheese until it becomes smooth

11. Slowly add the whole milk and heavy cream

12. Don't stop mixing

13. Whisk the eggs, two at a time

14. Squeeze the moisture out of the spinach

15. Break the feta and add it to the mixture

16. Stir in with the salt and pepper, cheddar, scallions, spinach, and parmesan

17. Don't turn off the oven after the crust finishes baking

18. Pour the filling on top of the crust

19. Bake the quiche for about 25 minutes until the crust becomes golden-brown and the filling is set

20. Leave it for about 10 minutes to cool down

Chickpea and Marjoram Frittata
Ingredients:
- 1 cup of cooked chickpeas
- 1 minced garlic clove
- 1 Spanish onion
- 4 eggs
- ½ cup of grated cheese
- ½ cup of milk
- Marjoram leaves
- Sea salt and black pepper

Instructions:
1. Slice the onion
2. Fry the sliced onions in butter or oil
3. Add the salt, pepper, and garlic
4. Now, remove it from the stove and thoroughly stir the herbs
5. Add the chickpeas
6. Keep stirring to combine the ingredients well
7. Pour the mixture into a pie dish
8. Now, add the grated cheese and the herbs
9. Beat the eggs
10. Stir in the milk
11. Then put them over the onions and chickpeas
12. Preheat the oven to 200 degrees
13. Put the mixture in the oven
14. Leave it to bake for about 20 minutes
15. When it is golden and firm, it means it is done

The great thing about making a frittata is that you can get creative with the ingredients and add whatever you want. For instance, if you are a vegetarian or a vegan, you can add rocket, corn kernel, or sweet potato. Meat lovers can also add salmon or ham. There are many spring vegetables to choose from, so play around and experiment with the ingredients you want.

Honey Fritter Cake

Ingredients:

- 2 eggs
- 2 teaspoons of cinnamon
- 2 tablespoons of honey (you can add more if you want to)
- 1 cup of milk
- 1 cup of self-rising flour

Instructions:

1. Using a fork, mix the milk, eggs, and honey together
2. Add the flour
3. Lightly mix the ingredients
4. Avoid over beating the ingredients, or they will become hard
5. Add the cinnamon (you can add other spices if you want)
6. Get a frying pan
7. Grease it lightly with butter or oil (preferable macadamia oil)
8. Heat the frying pan
9. Add spoonfuls of the mixture to the pan
10. Cook each side lightly

The right meal can make or break a festive celebration. If you are going to invite your friends and family to celebrate this magical Ostara with you, you need to choose dishes that reflect this beautiful occasion. Luckily, there are various fruits and vegetables waiting to be plucked and added to your ingredients at the beginning of spring. The recipes mentioned here will help you out when preparing meals for your first Ostara with your loved ones. Remember that you can always experiment with the ingredients. You are the chef here.

While preparing your meals, you should set intentions for the food you want to create. Setting intentions is a lot similar to praying but without formality. You choose the kind of experience you wish to have, which will help put you in the right direction. We cook almost every day, so it becomes more of a habit. We never really think beforehand about the kind of experience we want to have while cooking or our relationship with the food we are making.

Before you prepare your Ostara meal, get a pen and paper, and write down what you want to achieve from this meal: healing, nourishment, energy, or connecting with your family. Now take a look at what you wrote and choose the intention calling to you. For instance, if you hope that this meal will help you connect with your family, then set the intention "this meal will help me connect with my family" before preparing the meal. Setting an intention will help you choose the appropriate food and ingredients. It will also deepen your relationship with food because you'll see it as more than just a meal but as a method to help you achieve your goals.

Chapter 7: Magical Gardening

Ostara is a Wiccan holiday that marks the celebration of the return to life, renewal of the earth, and light. Being one of the eight Sabbats, Eostre represents spring and new beginnings. This time of the year marks the beginning of the farming cycle when farmers would begin to plant seeds. One way of celebrating Ostara or the renewal of the earth is to practice magical gardening.

The chapter discusses how you create garden charms to bless the soil in your garden, do seed blessings, and create magical fertilizers. It also highlights the instructions for creating the miniature greenhouse to grow Ostara herbs and other plants. The last section of the chapter provides a list of Ostara plants, herbs, and flowers. It also recommends magical ways to use each one.

Garden Charms

When preparing your magic garden, you should first consider blessing it with charms you'll bury in the soil. The following are some of the appropriate charms you can consider for your magic garden.

- Dried fruits preserved from the previous season
- Small pieces of apple to display the pentacle
- Solar symbols
- A Goddess figuring in wood, clay, or other organic materials
- Horns dedicated to the Horned God
- Whole eggs
- Yonic or phallic symbols
- Quartz crystals are associated with fertility and the energy of the Goddesses, such as Moss Agate, Rosophia, Gaia Stone, Citrine, Green Fluorite, Unakite, and others.

You must consecrate and bless your preferred items depending on your preferences. A quick way to bless a statue is to breathe life into it and make sure you do that with an intention. You can also perform a quick consecration with the charms, which you can bury at the corners of your garden. If you have a single charm, you can bury it at the center of your garden.

You must visualize the charms as providing the energy of fertility to the soil, promoting the growth of the plants, and delineating barriers that pests cannot cross. You can also consider other sympathetic and statuary charms like garden gnomes. This sympathetic magic is effective since it can attract nature spirits. You can also add a variety of garden decorations, including butterflies, bees, faeries, glass witch balls, wind chimes, and wreaths.

Old Magic

Other forms of old charm you can consider for your garden include broom leaping, dancing, or sex in groups or couples near the garden space. However, you should make your intention clear for embarking on these practices.

Deities

If you want to request blessings of deities in your garden, there are different options you can consider. Some of them include the following:

- Ceres
- Blodeuwedd
- Danu
- The Dagda
- Dionysus
- Demeter
- Freyr
- Kokopelli
- Isis
- Hermes (god of boundaries)
- Inari Okami
- Inanna/Ishtar
- Mars
- Kouzin Zaka
- Modron
- Meztli
- Osiris
- Pachamama
- Pomona
- Persephone
- Priapus

- Xochipilli
- Xochiquetzal

When you decide to use these deities in your garden, make sure you don't just randomly pick something. Before you choose any of these deities, it is better to do some research and learn something about their traditional offerings to help you make an informed decision. You should conduct background checks to see if there is anything that makes the deity odd. For example, the Mesoamerican deities used to be associated with human sacrifice, while Dionysus used to be known as driving people into cannibalism. Therefore, you must get an idea of what each deity represents before you get it.

Magical Fertilizer

Another vital component you should consider for your garden is magical fertilizer. There are different things you can sprinkle over your garden soil or mix with fertilizer or compost to promote growth in your garden. The following are some of the items you can consider.

- Broken eggshells, particularly Easter eggs
- Mead
- Consecrate wine
- Consecrated milk
- Handfasting or wedding cake
- Animal bones from meals (You can clean the bones first and draw magical symbols to bless them. You also need to enlist the influence of the animal spirits they belong to
- Consecrated food
- Yule tree remains
- Menstrual blood or semen (collect it using biodegradable material

You can also add some invocation as you prepare your magical fertilizer, like: "I call upon the earth's spirits."

Magical Gardening

When you have prepared all the fundamental tasks, the next step is to move to the fun part of magical gardening. This is a rewarding magical activity, but it involves some work, and plants do not grow randomly. You need to prepare the garden and the herbs you'll grow in your garden. You should consider various factors if you want to grow a successful magical garden.

Hardiness Zones

When you undertake a magical project, you should begin with non-magical things. In the case of preparing a garden, you should know the hardiness zone you are in. This includes the type of weather or climate in your area. You can use a map to gain insight into the zone where you belong. The climate in your area will determine the types of plants you can grow in your area. Other plants perform well in dry climates, while others prefer wet conditions. Therefore, choose herbs and flowers that suit the climatic conditions in your area.

Soil Type

There are different types of soils, and they are suitable for various plants. Common soil types include loam, dry soil, clay, hard, crossroads dirt, and others. You should have your soil tested first if you plan to start gardening inside or outside your yard. Your Home depot or garden supply store can test your soil to determine its pH to suit what you want to plant. Depending on the soil type, you may need to mix an additive, and you should also know how the soil traps moisture. For instance, sandy soil does not hold moisture longer, and clay soil requires plants with strong roots to break it.

Little Sunshine

All plants require a certain amount of sunshine every day to enhance growth. Other plants require full sun in different climates, while others can thrive in cool conditions. You should ascertain that the area where you plan to place your plants receives sufficient light. Note that the afternoon sun is more intense than morning sunlight.

Make sure you choose the best location in your yard for your magical garden.

Determine the Purpose of Your Garden

You should determine the purpose of your garden like any other magical work. Define the reasons why you want to start a magical garden. Other people grow it to attract fairies, while others grow herbs to use in their workings. After you've determined your intention, you'll need to look for plants that fit your specific purpose. If you visit your local garden store, you'll find seed packs that match your specific theme.

Choose Your Seeds

When choosing your seeds, you need to remember if you'll keep them in a container or transplant them into your garden. You must do some research to determine the herbs that do well indoors or outdoors. If you buy heirloom seeds, you can regrow them the following year. GMO plants cannot produce seeds that you can use the following cropping season. If you want to create a green witch's paradise, you can consider strictly medicinal seeds. Apart from getting the desired seeds, you should also acquire pots to plant them, a pen and paper to write your intention, newspaper, or cardboard to lay on the floor if you want to grow your seeds inside.

Seeding for Success

When you acquire the preferred seeds, the next step is to plant them according to the instructions provided on the package. You should trust that your intention will succeed. If you want to plant outside, you need to create a small nursery for your seeds first. You must have a paper where you plot the growth stages of the plants until they mature. Have a map about how you'll plant the flowers or herbs and keep a timeline for transplanting them if you use an outside magic garden. There are different ideas you can consider when planning your magic garden.

You need to decorate your altar, home, or sacred space with the things that align with the Spring season. For instance, you can consider flowers like tulips, pussy willows, hyacinths, or anything from nature. Include colored eggs for fertility, citrine, and crystals such as rose quartz, green aventurine, aquamarine, and amethyst. If you want to use candles, green, pink, and yellow colors will be great.

Cleanse and Ground

When you prepare your nursery, you must cleanse and ground the space where you would like to plant the herbs or flowers. You can do this by smudging with incense or herbs or using your favorite essential oils such as rose, geranium, neroli, and lemon. Any material you use should pass through mist or smoke. Sit or stand, then start to create a connection with your breath. You should breathe slowly and consciously and make sure you feel your nervous system calming. Your body movement also needs to slow down when performing the cleansing and grounding ceremony.

You should meditate on your intention for your Spring magic garden, where you outline what you want to achieve. At this moment, you should feel your intention developing and growing inside your body. You should be ready to embody the creation you are making on this particular Equinox. You should ask for insight, clarity, and guidance. It is important to remain quiet so that answers can emerge from within. Write your intention down when you are clear about what you want to achieve.

Visualize

The next step is to hold your seeds and try to visualize your intention if it can come to fruition. You must not doubt your intention but feel the joy, excitement, peace, and pride. You should also feel the energy of wholeness, which you should use to feed the seeds, so they bear fruit. Remember to whisper your intention to the seeds as if you are sharing a secret.

Bless Your Soil

It is essential to bless the soil first, and you can achieve this by establishing communication with it. Dip your fingers into the earth and feel its liveness. This will transfer waves of gratitude and blessings into the soil where you'll plant your seeds. Blessing the soil also helps promote the fruition of your plants.

Plant Your Seeds

When you have blessed the soil, you can move on to plant your intention. Place the written intention at the bottom of the pot. Do the same if you use crystal and cover it with soil. Choose the day that corresponds with your intention before planting your seeds. You can cast your circle around your garden and call different elements of deities to help your garden thrive. You can also create a garden guardian, which you can place among the plants.

Another crucial thing you should know is that plants love music. Therefore, you can play your favorite music when growing the plants to raise power that will enhance growth. When planting seeds in the nursery, make sure to place them in a way that will allow them to sprout easily. You must push them to the depth in the soil as stated on the packet. While planting your seeds, you need to keep on stating your intention. Tell the seeds your intention to make them feel loved and appreciated. This also helps you transfer the energy you have requested into the seeds.

Once the seeds are planted, walk around the area, and introduce your guardian to the seeds and your intention. Your guardian in spiritual form should also tell you where you should plant the seedlings once they germinate. Keep on watering the seeds and sending gratitude and blessings to your seeds. Gently water the seeds to ensure you do not disturb them.

Transplant the Seeds

If you intend to grow your plants in an outdoor garden, you should transplant them when they are ready. When the enchanted seedlings are established and are free from the risk of weather elements such as frost, you can plant them in your garden. You can replant your written intention in the garden if you feel like doing so. Another important aspect to consider is having a diagram when planting the seedlings in the garden. Ensure they have enough space to grow and are not congested. As the plants grow, their foliage will also expand, and it can impact growth if there is no space.

Care and Trust

As indicated earlier, you need to choose the best site for the garden in your yard. The plants in the garden should get sufficient sunlight. You can also add crystals in the soil or around the pots to enhance the growth of your plants. You must check on the newly grown plants in your garden daily so they grow with your intentions and goals. Make sure your seedlings don't get excessive water since this can impact growth. You must water them as instructed by professionals.

Be Patient

We don't know how the plants will grow in most cases, but we are certain they will. At this stage, you don't need to focus on how the plants will grow but on the outcome. Nature does not hurry, but it will bear fruit in everything grown. You must have trust and patience. All you need to do is take time to nurture your growing plants and your intentions. Try to revisit your goals every day and send love to your planted seeds. Visualize your goal and send gratitude to the plants in the garden.

Like any other earth magic, plants in your magical garden take time to grow and bloom. You may also encounter setbacks that can impact your intentions. For instance, weather elements can impact your garden in different ways, but you need to find ways to address the challenges to salvage your plants. Insects can also attack your garden, so you need to take appropriate steps to control them. In some instances, you'll realize that other plants can thrive while others simply die no matter how you try to look after them well.

How to Create a Miniature Greenhouse to Plant Ostara Herbs and Plants

If you do not have appropriate outdoor space for your outside garden, you can create a miniature greenhouse. If it is too cold outside to plant seeds outside, you can get started indoors, where your seedlings can thrive. You must plan ahead of time to know what you want to plant. It is essential to give the plants a head start to sprout ahead of schedule. When the warmer weather finally arrives, you can transfer the plants to their intended space.

You can make a small indoor greenhouse, and you'll need the following items to make it.

- Disposable baking pan consisting of a plastic lid
- Seeds
- Potting soil
- Small peat pots

You should start by preparing your baking pan. These baking pans are available in grocery stores, and they come in black or foil. Foil pans can reflect light better than the black ones, so try to get these if possible. If you use a black pan, make sure you line it using an aluminum foil sheet. This sheet will help reflect light so that it does not affect the plants.

You also need to poke holes at the bottom of the pan for drainage. Make sure the holes are not too big so the pan can retain some water and moisture. And make sure the holes are not too small, as this can lead to excessive moisture, which can cause root rotting. You can start with a few holes and add more later, depending on the growth rate of the plants.

When you have prepared your peat pots, fill them with potting soil and line them to fit inside the baking pan. Place a seed in the soil inside each pot and cover it. When you place seeds in each pot, mix everything with water. Place the lid on the baking pan and put it on a sunny window. When the interior of the baking pan warms up in the sun, condensation will develop on the lid. The heat trapped from the sun and condensation will aid the seeds sprouting inside the peat pots placed in the baking pan.

Do not remove the lid to allow the plants to grow. If you want to remove the lid to water the plants, make sure you do it over a short period. You can watch your seeds begin to sprout, and this can take a few days or weeks, depending on the type of plants inside. When you feel your seedlings are ready, you can transplant them into your garden. You only need to place the peat pot with the seedling into the soil. However, make sure to arrange your peat pots strategically so that the plants are not congested, which can stunt growth.

Magical Gardening Plants and their Purpose

There are different plants you can consider for your magic garden, and they can be used for various purposes. Other herbs and flowers thrive indoors. The following are some plants you can grow inside your home and their purpose.

- **Rosemary**: This plant offers cleansing and protective qualities, and you can use them for magical purposes. If you want to purify your home, burn the dried leaves, and the smoke can do wonders.

- **Basil:** This plant brings happiness, prosperity, and love. Having it in your home in different states can help you enjoy a happy life.
- **Oregano:** Another plant that promotes tranquility, joy, and health. You can use it in different forms to enjoy its immense benefits.
- **Thyme:** This is a herb that promotes self-confidence and courage. When you burn it, it wards off negativity, and it can also bring good fortune.
- **Mint:** It helps improve verbal communication and adds power to your prayer and words. When you take the herb orally, it can break negativity, misfortune, and bad luck. You can cook with these herbs, use them to make tea, or perform other forms of magic.

On the other hand, the common witchy herbs you can grow in the garden include the following:

- **Mugwort:** This is a wonderful plant that promotes lucid and psychic dreams. It is good to dry and smudge with.
- **Calendula:** It promotes love and joyful energy and is amazing for making salves.
- **Rue:** This garden plant consists of protective and cleansing qualities. If you are looking for protection against unforeseen elements, you can use this plant.
- **Lavender:** Promotes quality sleep, calms your nerves, and offers relaxation. The plant also produces a nice scent with healing and soothing properties to the mind.
- **Yarrow:** It is used for divination and to protect the auric field. If you want to know something about the future, you can use this plant. The herb gives you insight into different things you can encounter.
- **Garden Sage:** This plant is used for protection and wisdom. It can help you make meaningful decisions in

your life. It is great for teas and culinary purposes in different dishes.

Magical gardening is one way of celebrating Ostara, and it symbolizes the renewal of the earth. You should consider different things like creating garden charms, blessing the soil in your garden, and creating magical fertilizer. However, gardening takes time, commitment, and work, just like loving someone. You may not always achieve your desired goals, but you need to keep trying. Instead, you should learn from your mistakes if you are concerned about achieving your goals. You should also consider several things when preparing your garden, as highlighted in this section. The next chapter focuses on prayers, invocations, and chants.

Chapter 8: Prayers, Invocations, and Chants

Besides the craft projects you can participate in while preparing for the arrival of spring, you can also get in the spirit of Ostara by reading and reciting some prayers, invocations, and chants. Preparing for such a momentous occasion can be stressful - and there is a lot to think of, especially if this is your first time celebrating Ostara. By reciting some Ostara-related chants, everything can become much brighter. You'll become full of energy to do everything you need to prepare for spring. And by singing some upbeat poems and chants while preparing Ostara dishes or decorations, your move will improve even more. The time will fly, and your tasks will be done before you even realize it.

If you have children, this is the easiest way to involve them in the process - and by doing so, you'll have even more fun. If you don't, you can still persuade fellow witches or friends and family to join you. For those welcoming the Spring Equinox as solitary practitioners, singing Ostara chants can be a great way to keep their minds filled with jovial thoughts during this period. These promote positivity and fertility in magic and professional life alike.

If you want to draw magic from the awakening nature or Eostre herself, you'll need to invoke them with chants and prayers. Since they require the focusing of your mind, chanting invocations and prayers for Ostara is the best way to get in tune with the true spirit of this sabbat. Prayers work best if recited in front of the altar or during meditation - when you are in a relaxed state of mind. They can help you form a deeper connection with nature and the spiritual world, particularly at this time of the year. By celebrating this season, you are bestowing a great honor to the greatest forces in the universe. In turn, they will allow you to synchronize your magic with Ostara's.

Preparing for Chanting Prayers, Invocations, and Chants

There isn't much preparation for chanting Ostara poems and songs, except learning the words and the meaning of each poem or song. After that, you'll be ready to break into your favorite Ostara song whenever the mood strikes you. Or you can organize a reading session with your fellow witches or social circle and read the poems aloud.

Now, with prayers, the situation is a little bit different. Prayers can invoke the most powerful magic on the exact day of the Spring Equinox. If you can, this is the best time to chant them. If you have decided to learn them just shortly before the arrival of this date - and you aren't able to recite the prayer just yet (or aren't confident enough to do so), you may do it after the spring has officially arrived. You are free to decide what feels right for you at a time, so you can determine when to start saying the prayer of your choice. Most prayers aren't for one-time use only, and you can repeat them as many times and whenever you feel like doing it. That being said, it's not advised to recite Ostara prayers with intent before the arrival of spring. No matter how you may be tempted by the warm weather and the bright sun, it's best to wait and only practice the prayer. If you are really inspired by seeing nature, come back to life, you may chant some invocations to natural spirits or Eostre. They won't mind being honored by you seeking them out and asking them to help you throughout the year that comes. Prayers, however, often have very different purposes. While they can also be used for asking for guidance, more often than not, they contain praises and words of gratitude. These have the purpose of further ensuring the help from the entity the prayer is directed to. This is another compelling reason for reciting them only when their magic is most powerful.

Stay still for a couple of more minutes after prayer, and reflect on how you feel. If you have used a smaller candle, you may let it burn out, and if you have used a larger one, save it for your next prayer. It's also a good idea to keep a symbol of the subject of your prayers nearby after your prayer. This will infuse it with your energy, making it more powerful for using them in spells.

Prayer for Ostara

On Ostara, the time of birth and rebirth,
Help me reconnect with what comes to life,
Help me receive the energizing magic of Nature and Earth,
So, when they come alive, I can do the same.
Help me recharge my magic,
Through the fertile energy that's taking over,
Until it becomes one with me,
And mine become one with it.
I am ready to accept a new path
So, bless me with a new life
And help me spread it around me.
Prayer for The Revival of Nature
Now that the deep sleep of winter is fading
And the hand of the frost losses
Nature may be revived once more.

May it come alive again,
And return to the fertile land.
Bringing spring on its way,
As it warms and the snow melts away.
The too soil warms and comes to life
Sprouting grass and flowers alike.
Let all life awaken and the earth reborn
So, spring can work its magic anew.

Ostara Garden Blessing

While the earth still looks dark and cold,
New life has already sprouted down below.
May our gardens be fertile and full come harvest,
May we have rain but be free of pests.
We welcome the nourishing Sun,
When our crops need energy, may it come,
May our soil be blessed now,
So, it becomes fruitful in autumn.
Let our garden thrive
Blessed be.

A Poem about Ostara

Ostara is the reflection of sunlight on the leaves,
It is in the music of the streams,
It is in the scent of blossoming flowers
It is in our dreams as they become reality.
Ostara can transform our sorrow into joy,
As it makes the darkness of the winter
into a warm spring day,
Everything bad fades away.
Ostara is what brings the change,
And grants new life a chance.

With all the new insects and birds chirping away,
Nature will never twice be the same,
They dance as plants and snakes follow,
And our life will never be shallow.
Praising the Goddess of Fertility
We hail to you, oh goddess of spring,
You who bring the warm winds,
Make flowers bloom and animals stir,
Help the soil awake so we can plant the seeds.
We praise you, oh goddess of fertility,
As we know that through the cycles of life,
You'll bring us a good harvest and bounty.
Only you can make us fertile in our work,
Through our hands and hearts.
We praise you for all your blessings,
And the hope you bring us,
We pray that you cover the land
So, this year can too come to a fruitful end.

Greeting Eostre

As we watch nature shed its winter cloak,
We welcome to the warmth that follows,
So, we greet you, Eostre, lady of Spring.
With our joyful hearts,
We dance at your arrival,
Goddess of the early sunrise.
We welcome the lively colors
And the blessing that follows
In abundance may we grow,
So, we can prosper now and tomorrow.
Grant us a mindful eye

So, we don't miss
The chance to thrive.
In you, we see the promise of a better tomorrow
Blessed be now and forever.

Prayer for Honoring the Goddesses of Spring

As the new life returns to the earth,
Everything is preparing to bloom,
And appear once more out of the nourishing soil.
So, we welcome you in,
Beautiful goddesses of spring,
Eostre, Flora, Cybele, and Persephone.
We see your magic in the trees,
You work in the soil that brings,
Flowers and grains,
And we know whom to be grateful to,
when it rains.

Goddess of Ostara Invocation

The Goddess of Ostara comes with the spring
Cloaked in the sunlight, she melts the snow,
Green leaves, flowers, and awakened animals,
She brings many gifts to the revived earth.
The Goddess of Ostara comes with the spring,
Fair Maiden, we seek to welcome you in.
We plant our seeds now, oh Goddess of spring,
And we will reap what we have sown in the autumn wind,
We ask you to guide us with your light touch,
As your kindness envelops us.
When she comes, she offers us the sacred egg,
Providing birth, fertility, and a circle that's complete,
The Goddess of Ostara comes with the spring,

Fair Maiden, we seek to welcome you in.

A Hopeful Chant for Ostara

Ostara, when springtime comes,
And when nature transforms,
Everything is new, and everything grows,
Everything will change, and we might cry,
But this day will be filled with hope no matter why.
A Chant for Celebrating Ostara
When the wheel of the year turns,
And the long daylight returns,
Here comes Ostara, the forebearer of spring.
As the Sun is regaining its strength,
The time with sowing will now be spent.
The goddess now bestows her blessings onto our lands,
She replenishes our sources,
So come winter, we have food again in our hands.

Creating Your Own Dedications to Ostara

Lastly, you should keep in mind that magic is highly personal. The power comes from within you, and it changes over time. If you are at the beginning of your magical journey, you may need to rely on existing prayers and chants for your spells and rituals. As you become wise in the ways of a witch and learn how to evoke more power, you'll be able to create your own magical aids. Ostara is one of the largest and most enchanting sabbats, which can also provide you with the most inspiration. Nothing can help you more in creating your own dedication to Ostara than observing as nature sheds its winter cloak and comes to life around you.

- **Decorating Your Altar:** You may add a potted plant to keep yourself close to nature at all times. Crystals, symbols, and candles that speak to you about nature are all helpful additions. Vivid spring colors usually help boost the vibe, but if you feel that you would rather use white, that's fine as well.

• **Learning the Symbols:** Ostara has more symbols than just the eggs and the rabbits it's known for. There are also seeds, snakes, wheat, and literally everything that comes from nature and may symbolize fertility. Learning them and using them in your practice is another great way to celebrate this sabbat.

• **Creating a Prayer:** Write your own prayer for Ostara and recite it every day in front of your altar. Light a candle while doing as the flames help carry the magic.

• **Getting Crafty:** There are plenty of craft projects you can do for Ostara, so you should have no trouble finding the ideal ones for you. Some are better suited for solitary witches, while others are great for families with children. Don't forget to add some of your creations to your altar.

• **Writing a Poem:** Even if you are welcoming spring on your own, this doesn't mean you can't get into the spirit of Ostara by coming up with a poem or chant of your own. And if you have children, they will love singing your Ostara songs while preparing for the sabbat.

• **Practicing Mindfulness:** While the spring is known for its abundance of activity, sometimes the only way to enjoy this is to slow down a bit by yourself. Find the closest piece of nature, stop for a couple of minutes, and do some mindfulness exercises while observing it.

• **Trying Out New Activities:** Seeking out an activity you always wanted to try will energize you, which will have a positive impact on your magic as well. Becoming committed to this activity during this time of the year ensures that you receive everything you need from Ostara.

Chapter 9: Spells and Rituals for Solitaries

Pagan traditions vary widely, and they focus strongly on rituals, spells, and magick to create change in individuals through physical actions and prayer. Practitioners may use multiple sources to follow a particular Pagan tradition. Other traditions include Wicca, a kind of religious witchcraft, Druidry, non-Wiccan religious witchcraft, and feminist Goddess worship. The rituals and spells mainly focus on observing natural cycles like seasonal changes, honoring a deity or deities, or celebrating passage rites such as birth, marriage, and death.

A participant is involved physically in the rituals that often include chanting, drumming, and dancing. While other rituals and spells are practiced in groups, solitary or individual practitioners can also do the same. This chapter discusses the spells and rituals for Solitaries in Ostara. It discusses different types of Wiccan and druid rituals and spells.

Solitary Practice

Although some Pagans practice in groups, many are solitaries implying they practice alone. Many pagans identify as solitary, and they only gather with small groups for special occasions. Most of them prefer to worship in private homes or outdoors. The solitary practitioners are known as Neo-pagans who follow diverse religions such as Wicca, traditional reconstructionism, and witchcraft. The following are some of the spells and rituals for solitaries.

Ostara Ritual

To perform this ritual, you need to use the season's symbols to decorate your altar. Spring represents fertility in the world, so you should decorate the altar with appropriate seasonal symbols. For instance, you can consider the colors you see in nature during this time, like plump tulips, daffodils, crocuses, and green shoots. You also need to include symbols of young animals like chicks, lambs, rabbits, and calves since they symbolize Ostara.

On top of decorating the altar, you can also perform the ritual outside early in the morning, where you can reconnect with the earth. You'll need a bowl of milk, three candles (one green, one yellow, and one purple), and a bowl of sugar or honey. The first thing is to focus on the air around where you should inhale deeply to smell if there is a change in the season. Since spring is a season of rebirth, the air will consist of a smell of fresh green grass, earthly and rainy aroma.

The next step is to light the green candle that symbolizes the blossoming earth and chant a few praising the coming of a new season. You need to light the yellow candle next, which represents the sun. As you light this candle, you must say a few words in appreciation of the warmth and light provided by the sun. The sun warms the land, promoting the growth of plants. Finally, you must light a purple candle representing the Divine force in our lives. This can be a god or goddess, and this candle stands for the things we cannot understand in our lives but are sacred. Focus on the Divine aspect of the candle as you chant something.

You should take a moment to meditate, focusing on the three flames before you and considering what they symbolize. You also need to determine how you fit between the three components: the sun, earth, and Divine symbolized by the three burning candles. Finally, mix the honey and milk, and pour the mixture around the altar as an offering to the earth. You may wish to say something as you present your offering. Stand for about one minute facing the altar once you make your offering and feel the sun on your face and the cool earth beneath your feet.

Grounding or Earth Meditation

Grounding meditation is one crucial and simple daily practice for many Pagans. It helps you connect with the energy of the earth and maintain emotional and physical balance. You must find a place to sit quietly – and make sure the sun is shining and nothing disturbs you from performing this meditation. Ensure that you locate an outdoor place where you can connect with everything that represents the earth. The practice of divination is another example of grounding meditation where you ask about the day ahead. Other Pagans use Tarot cards or runes while others consult astrology to gain access to sources of spiritual knowledge. Others can look for connections with the natural world through interactions with plants, animals, water, and wind to understand different patterns of the local environment.

Making an Eggshell Fertility Talisman

To make this talisman, you'll need:

- A needle and thread
- A small green circle cloth
- Eggshells
- A piece of paper with an image of your goal
- Some fertility herbs like carrot, bistort, nuts, wheat, rice, myrtle, barley, rye, acorns, pine cones, cedar, juniper, turnips, honeysuckle, and lemongrass

You can also include geodes or holey stones associated with fertility. Infuse all the ingredients with your desire for a baby. Place them in the green cloth and sew them. Holding the talisman between your belly and hands, begin to chant and ask your goddess for a baby. You should wear your talisman around your belly as much as you can. You can renew your intent by chanting appropriate words related to conceiving a baby.

Other Forms of Egg Magick

There are also other types of egg magick you can consider making positive changes in your life. For instance, you can sweep hard-boiled eggs from outside the house to the interior using a broom. This ritual is specifically meant to bring fertility and abundance. You can also use brown eggs to perform magick that will help in animal husbandry. The eggs will protect your livestock against diseases and provide healing power. Brown eggs also help ease the pets when giving birth. The other magic you can perform is to bury a rotten egg near a crossroad, which will cause abundance to shift from the enemy to you.

To ensure you have sufficient food in your home during winter, bury one egg at each corner of the cardinal point of your yard. This magick also helps keep your family safe by offering protection powers. Before you begin spring planting, make sure you bury some eggs in your garden. Decorated eggshells hanging from trees surrounding a particular place provide blessings of abundance.

Magick

Many Pagans exercise magick, which is different from the stage or other forms of fanciful magic in novels. In Paganism, magick is viewed as a spiritual practice that functions like prayer, and it comes with a more physical component. It aims to create change within an individual and in the world. When you practice magick, you should start by stating a clear intention and raising the required energy to support it.

You can achieve this through dancing and chanting, breath exercises, or concentration. The energy will be released into the world or an object that serves as the focus of the intention. The object can be a piece of jewelry, a candle, or any item on the altar. Pagans feel that magick should include a practical component to be successful. For instance, you need to complete an application for a successful job magick.

Candle Rituals

Pagans often perform a variety of rituals daily to strengthen their spirituality. Other rituals are simple since they only involve lighting a candle in the dark and meditating on the flame. You can give a cup of water to your ancestors and say a prayer. A verbal ritual or spoken intention is believed to be very powerful. It can bring change to the Pagan's life if properly said. You need to choose your words carefully if you want to achieve your life goals.

Personal Cleansing

The first thing you should do is to build an altar if you want to do personal cleansing. This is a sacred workplace, or a place of divinity used by Pagans to perform rituals in their homes. An altar can be in any convenient location inside your home or outside if your yard is big. Your altar should have ritual tools, natural objects, photographs of the dead, or other items of beauty and personal power. You can undertake a healing or personal cleansing at the altar, or you can present an offering of a deity. You can also make a herbal charm or meditate at your altar. Looking at the altar will remind you of your spiritual life.

Spiritual Cleansing

Spiritual cleansing is another spell you can perform to make your heart spiritually clean and healthy. It is essential to draw closer to God, who can do the spiritual cleansing since we cannot do it. Apart from asking God to cleanse your heart, you also need to cleanse your body from within. For instance, you can deep clean your mouth and remove negativity and pessimism. You should train your mouth not to say bad things. This also involves the decision to refrain from arguing or complaining.

Spiritual cleansing also involves the removal of dirty things from your mind. Garbage in your mind affects the way you think, so feed it with the word of God. When you renew your mind, you can enjoy inner peace, which will help you live happily. Make sure you clean all the hidden areas since concealed sin can destroy your peace or health. Another important step you can take to cleanse yourself is to release bitterness and unforgiveness.

If you keep bitterness, it will look like baggage you'll become too familiar with but not aware of how it might be hindering your life. Similarly, you should learn to get rid of anger, rage, slander, and brawling. Instead, learn to be compassionate and kind to other people. Open your life and allow the light of God to shine in your body. Other people are too serious about life, which can impact them in different ways. You must have some fun to relieve pressure.

A Cascarone Love Spell

Knocking someone on the head with a special egg called the cascarone is another way of blessing you. Cascarones consist of eggshells collected over several weeks before Easter and are hollowed out carefully. They are then filled with different substances and decorated. When the eggs are knocked on someone's head, the substances inside will shower blessings on the individual involved. The common items used as fillers include sage, lavender, flour or cornmeal, and perfumed herbs. While the idea is playful, this spell effectively makes magick and provides blessings to others.

To make cascarone eggs, you should empty them first, and you can do this by making small holes on both ends of the egg. Wash the shells with cold water and allow them to dry. Decorate the shells before you fill them. You can add herbs or confetti to fill the empty shells. Make sure you use a small kitchen funnel and be careful not to break the shell or make it full since it can cause discomfort when you know it on someone's head. When the eggs shells are full, seal them and store them in a cool and dry place while you wait for Ostara morning.

When you want to perform a cascarone love spell, follow the instructions highlighted above and fill the shells with magickal herbs such as yarrow, lavender, rose petals, apple blossom, willow, daisies, or rosemary. These herbs are commonly associated with attracting romantic love. As you create your cascarone, you need to visualize the contents as a love catalyst. This will make your desired lover notice you more than other people without impinging their desire to choose a preferred lover. You can shower the person you love with the cascarone on Ostara or break it in a flowing river while visualizing your intention being carried to your loved one's heart.

Use of Sacred Jewelry

Jewelry is another special tool you can use for your spells and rituals. The Wiccans usually wear jewelry consisting of pagan symbols like the pentacle, a five-pointed star. This pentacle is a symbol of life, and it reflects the union of different elements, including air, earth, fire, and water, with the spirit. However, the pentacle is often misrepresented and associated with evil in horror movies. Not all pagans use the pentacle.

Green Spells

Green spells are primarily concerned with healing and nurturing. They draw power from the earth and use flowers, herbs, and other plants as the source of spell ingredients. Nature also provides ritual content, and it is the most respected component by the witches. You can become a green witch if you have a gift of soothing and healing, are drawn to nature, and enjoy gardening as well as tending herbs and plants.

Solitary rituals and spells are mainly focused on celebrating the coming of the spring season, which symbolizes rebirth or new life. There are different types of spells you can perform alone, and you'll need certain elements to undertake them. However, your needs and aspirations will determine the rituals or spells you can perform. The next chapter focuses on spells and rituals for social pagans.

Chapter 10: Spells and Rituals for Social Pagans

There are different spells and rituals for social Pagans you can perform to celebrate Ostara, which marks the coming of springs and new life. The last chapter discussed the spells and rituals for solitaries, and this one discusses some complex spells and rituals since they will require a group to perform.

Ostara Rebirthing

This ritual involves rebirthing, and you can perform it as part of a group. Ostara is an excellent way to help you rededicate yourself to the gods celebrated in your tradition. There should be an Ostara altar and supplies such as a bowl of soil, a black sheet for each participant, incense, and a white candle to perform this rite. The High Priest or High Priestess (HP) is the only person who must be on the altar. Other members of the group should wait in another room until the HP calls them. If you are performing this rite outside, other participants should wait at a distance away from the altar. If you are called to cast the circle, you can do it as instructed.

The first person should wait outside the circle and be covered with a black sheet from head to toe to start the ritual. You can be nude under the sheet if the group permits. When the HP is ready, they will call the first person into the altar, create an opening in the circle as the participant enters, and close behind them. Still covered in the black sheet, the participant will kneel on the floor before the altar. The HP greets the member and says:

> Today is the time of the Spring equinox.
> Ostara is a time of equal parts, light and dark.
> Spring has arrived, and it is a time of rebirth.
> The planting season will soon begin, and
> life will form once more within the earth.
> As the earth welcomes new life and new beginnings,
> so can we be reborn in the light and love of the gods*.

Do you, (name), wish to experience the rebirth of spring and

step out of the darkness into the light?

The participant will then reply with an affirmative answer, and the HP collects salt from the altar and sprinkles it over the participant clad in a black sheet. The HP will say the following: "With the blessings of the earth, the life within the soil, you are reborn in the eyes of the gods." The HP will then take incense and pass it to the participant, chanting blessings of the air and asking knowledge and wisdom to be brought to the member.

The HP takes a burning candle and passes it to the participant, asking the burning fire of the spring sun to bring harmony and growth. They finally sprinkle water around the participant chanting something to the effect that water brings blessings and the darkness of winter be swept by the warm spring rains. The participant will slowly emerge from the black sheet when everything is done since this is a symbolic rebirth. When you move out of the black sheet, remember you are leaving behind your darkness and stepping into the light. You should take your time to reflect on the magic that will come with this ritual. The HP will welcome the participant, saying, "you have stepped into the bright area" and asking the gods to welcome you. There HP will repeat the ceremony on every member until they have been reborn. When everyone in the group has passed through the rebirthing process, they need to take time to meditate to get the balancing energy of Ostara. While meditating, you must think of the balance you wish to get in your life and consider how you'll work hard to find peace and harmony.

Stargazing

Stargazing is another rite performed by cosmic witches who largely focus on lunar energies to celebrate Ostara. This spell helps protect people against celestial events, and their practice is active even though they use star signs and birth charts. They use their knowledge to seek changes instead of just reciting what is in the public domain. If you are drawn to the skies, you can perform stargazing with other people.

Ostara Ritual for a Coven

A coven is a group of witches comprising practitioners who gather for rituals such as celebrating sabbats or Ostara. The number of people involved in these groups usually varies, although many believe 13 to be ideal. Their meeting place is called a covenstead. Any group consisting of less than three members is known as a "working couple" regardless of the gender of the people involved. When a coven becomes too big, it can be unmanageable, and it can be split. A High Priest and High Priestess jointly lead the covens, although some ceremonies are led by only one of them.

The practice of Wicca coven rituals is based on the notion of getting into contact with nature and worshiping a goddess or a god. The practice also involves using magic to celebrate the wheel of the year. This ritual involves the presentation of deities to the goddess.

The Wiccans will use the ceremony to perform white magic that positively impacts life, not black magic.

Dance and Laugh Together

Ostara comes with a childlike kind of playfulness and fun. Dancing is not only exciting, but it helps magnetize blessings and gives you joy wherever you go. You must dance while barefoot and outdoors with others. Make sure you laugh at the wildness and silliness of the entire activity. You'll realize that dancing and laughing will fill you with the vibrant, buoyant, and springtime vibration that will energize you and make positive changes to your life. It is essential to ensure that you do this as a group to enjoy the benefits of this fun ritual to the fullest.

A Theatrical Ostara Ritual

The women's Ostara ritual aims to bring back spring and create a balance between life and death, day and night, and light and dark. The ritual involves different things, and it comes with a lot of activity in the center. Therefore, you should make sure you set your altar to the side so that it does not disturb the movement of people. The following are some of the activities you can expect before the ritual.

- **Dyeing Hard-Boiled Eggs** - Involves an egg hunt, which means there should be enough eggs for each member. Hide both plastic and real eggs before the ritual around the area where you'll conduct the rite.
- You may also need to prepare lyrics before the rite if you prefer using many songs and chants.
- If you want to play with puppets, make them in advance or assign the roles to participants if you want to have actors before the ritual.
- You can also make "spring fortunes" that are enough for each participant. You need to place these fortunes together with small chocolate eggs and candy-like jelly into plastic eggs.

When you have prepared the activities to perform before the ritual, you should also list the items you want people to bring to the ritual. The following are some of the required things for the ritual.

- Spring items like flowers, eggs, baby animal figures, budding twigs, and plants are required to decorate the altar.
- Musical instruments, particularly drums and rattles
- A walking stick, rain stick, or other items that can be used to wake the earth
- Dark cloak to cast off or festive clothes

The next thing is to create a sacred space where the ritual will be performed. Children and adults attend the ceremony, so it is important to create an efficient circle if many people attend the ritual. The space is purified by having two people walk the perimeter, wafting incense, sprinkling water and salt. The priestess can cast the circle with words, or a popular chant is used. When the ritual space is ready, the next step is to perform different rituals.

Awaken the Earth

The first ritual is to awaken the earth, and this can be done with little help. When the circle is cast, there may be a need to push it out to cover the entire area. The participants will walk around the yard to mark the beginning of the ritual. If some people show up with walking sticks, they can use them to tap the earth as they walk around. This is meant to wake up the earth. Everyone is encouraged to play their drum or shake the rattle. The participants will sing and chant, "And she will rise," as the awakening process continues. This song is fun but rousing, and it encourages mother earth to wake up. The participants will chant that "the earth is a woman is a woman, and she will wake up." The point of awakening the earth is to encourage spring energy to rise.

Awaken the Young Goddess and God

If there are kids around, they will become the center of attention in the process of awakening the young sun goddess and god after winter. If the young ones are timid to do this, a couple of adults can be requested to perform the task. The pair will lie in the center of the circle with a blanket or dark cloaks on them. The members will sing Whispers of Spring repeatedly to awaken the young god or goddess.

The couple in the center will finally spring up and cast their dark cloaks off. They will tell the participants that it is time to cast off the winter blanket, and everyone will throw away their winter coats in a typical fashion. Festive clothing is then revealed, accompanied by cheering and fun fare. This ritual is an excellent way to involve young children for them to understand its significance from a tender age. The rite does not require speaking but just acting to awaken the goddess. The song Whispers of Spring works perfectly well for this ritual, and it sounds magical when a group of people sings it in unison.

This is a nice way to involve some of the littlest kids, as it doesn't require speaking, just acting out the process of waking up. If you don't happen to have the (out of print) song, Whispers of Spring works just as well if you do it as spoken word. It sounds very magical when a whole group whispers it together in unison.

Conduct Some Spring Cleaning

Spring cleaning is one of the easiest rituals you can perform to celebrate Ostara. This simple ritual involves collective cleaning by people who don't honor the sabbats but clean their homes at the start of spring. Physical cleaning is a great way of removing stagnant energy from your home, impacting you to start afresh. When you clean your home, you are symbolically eliminating old things and paving the way for the new. This will give you a new lease on life, and the exercise brings joy and satisfaction.

YOu can infuse your cleansing floor wash with pine needles and rosemary to purify the energy while removing dirt and debris from your floor. You can also sprinkle black salt to absorb negative energy before sweeping your home. When you finish cleaning the place, you can use sage to smoke cleanse all stagnant energy.

Take Nature Walk

Getting outdoors is the best thing you can do after a long cold spell. Since Ostara is more about the fertility of the earth, you must find an appropriate park where you can take some nature walks to observe new plant life and growth. Walking as a group, try to watch for animal activity, especially the rabbits and birds. The fun thing you can do with your kids is to walk around with them and let them show you signs of spring. You can also help them create a bird feeder to attract birds to your home. This exercise is good since it helps you celebrate spring as a group where you learn and share different things about new life.

Spring is the time of the year that symbolizes new life and rebirth. During this time, new life returns, and the theme of resurrection is dominant. Depending on your tradition, it can be observed that there are different spells and rituals for social pagans that are used to celebrate Ostara. The celebrations mark the arrival of spring and the fertility of the land, which characterizes agricultural changes.

Conclusion

Ostara is a magical time of light and balance in the universe. It is a pagan holiday that has morphed and transformed itself throughout the years, celebrated by Wiccans, but it also remains a touchstone of Druidry and paganism. Most people worldwide also celebrate this time of year, if only by another name to better suit newer theological or ideological frameworks. However, that has not robbed this time of the year of its joyfulness or color. In fact, it has only grown in popularity over time, and the renaissance or renewed interest in Wicca has only underscored this fact.

This book has provided an easy-to-follow guide for the various rituals and ceremonies attached to this wonderful holiday, and there are even more you can research and discover once you devote more time to your practice. Setting up an Ostara Altar is, of course, key, but there are other fun things you may consider exploring should you have the wherewithal. For example, there are wonderful nursery rhymes for kids to help them become more excited about the holiday. One called the "banishing ritual of the chocolate rabbit" is a funny rite for kids to practice. Still, it's one that the whole family can enjoy doing together if that's something you're interested in pursuing. Ostara magic is mostly wholesome and accessible for people of all ages, so you can get little pagans involved if that is a plan you're interested in exploring later on.

Part of the point of going through this guide is to underscore the historical significance of this holiday, render the complex rituals around it more accessible, and encourage serious study of other aspects of Wicca. One way to help you enrich your practice is to explore the folklore pertaining to the Ostara. Many tales regarding serpents, egg magic, spring flowers, and the bunny rabbit are worth your while. These stories divine the important symbolism contained within seemingly benign objects or beings - a daffodil, the March hare - and delve deeper into their history. If you thought the Ostara was simply the pagan prototype for Easter, then you are sorely mistaken. If you love celebrating St. Paddy's day, you might be surprised to learn about more connections between the Ostara and that holiday. The former doesn't have sole proprietary influence over the ever-elusive four-leaf clover. In fact, it is mentioned in some of the earliest known Ostara rituals.

So, now that you know everything you need to know about Ostara and how to honor this ancient tradition, you should feel empowered enough to do more historical research and readings. Also, no Ostara is complete without a true feast, so you might as well get the table ready and pay tribute to the coming of spring. Eggs, painted or not, are more than welcome, as is a fresh salad of spring greens and hot cross buns. Commercial treats aren't shunned either, so if you want to buy a bunch of colorful marshmallow Peeps, then go ahead! Just remember the origins of this unique celebration, and do your best to honor the arrival of spring.

Made in the USA
Las Vegas, NV
10 March 2024

87003427R00083